# Emetophobia

*of related interest*

**Free Yourself from Emetophobia**
**A CBT Self-Help Guide for a Fear of Vomiting**
*Alexandra Keyes and David Veale*
ISBN 978 1 78775 331 0
eISBN 978 1 78775 332 7

**Facing Mighty Fears About Throwing Up**
*Dawn Huebner, PhD*
*Illustrated by Liza Stevens*
ISBN 978 1 78775 925 1
eISBN 978 1 78775 926 8
*Part of* Dr. Dawn's Mini Books About Mighty Fears *series*

**The A-Z Guide to Exposure**
**Creative ERP Activities for 75 Childhood Fears**
*Dawn Huebner, PhD and Erin Neely, PsyD*
ISBN 978 1 83997 322 2
eISBN 978 1 83997 323 9

# EMETOPHOBIA

*Understanding and Treating Fear of Vomiting in Children and Adults*

## Dr David Russ
## and Anna S. Christie

Foreword by Dr David Veale

**Jessica Kingsley Publishers**
London and Philadelphia

First published in Great Britain in 2023 by Jessica Kingsley Publishers
An imprint of Hodder & Stoughton Ltd
An Hachette Company

1

A CIP catalogue record for this title is available from the
British Library and the Library of Congress

ISBN 978 1 83997 657 5
eISBN 978 1 83997 658 2

Printed and bound in Great Britain by CPI Group (UK) Ltd, Croydon CR0 4YY

Jessica Kingsley Publishers' policy is to use papers that are natural,
renewable and recyclable products and made from wood grown in
sustainable forests. The logging and manufacturing processes are expected
to conform to the environmental regulations of the country of origin.

Jessica Kingsley Publishers
Carmelite House
50 Victoria Embankment
London EC4Y 0DZ

www.jkp.com

Anna S. Christie

*For Jemima—you are a beautiful, amazing person.*

*May you always live in hope.*


Dr David Russ

*For Lindsey—your struggle inspired the cure for so many.*

# Contents

# Acknowledgments

## Anna S. Christie

My thanks go out to the amazing people who helped me in my journey through emetophobia. These include my good friend and therapist Peter Silin, without whom I would never have had the courage to do what I did, as well as my long-time therapist Geoffrey Carr whose brilliance, knowledge, skill, and compassion not only brought me through emetophobia, but also taught me what it is to be human.

I am extremely grateful to the people of Richmond Hospital who took a chance on me and allowed me to function as an assistant chaplain during my recovery in 2003 and for the following five years. These include the hospital chaplain, Rev. John Unrau, who supervised my work, and a group of nurses without whom I would not have made it through, in particular Beryl Mackleston and Cathie Colpitts.

I would also never have recovered nor been able to write this book without the help of the online emetophobic community. There are literally tens of thousands of you whom I have read about and written to since 2000. At first you helped me feel not alone in my struggle. Margaret, from the Netherlands, your pictures got me started on exposure therapy way back then and I've never forgotten you. John and Rich, owners of the International Emetophobia Society forum, thank you for your investment of time and money to help others. I have been so privileged to be a part of that forum, as well as several Facebook groups and pages. Thank you as well to the people on Instagram, Reddit, Twitter, and TikTok who have shared your stories. My podcast has been a wonderful experience, but I could not have even started it without volunteers from these communities willing to be interviewed.

To my clients whom I have helped: may God bless you with rich, wonderful lives full of joy and purpose. To those whom I could not help: I pray that there will soon be thousands of other therapists who can help you, with knowledge I may have gained after our time together. This is a highly treatable disorder, so don't be afraid to try again.

To my husband of 40 years, Charlie, who has worked tirelessly long after he should have retired to support me walking away from a great career with pension and benefits to starting all over at age 50 as a psychotherapist. Your honesty in all things, the love you have for your family and your generosity are incredible. I love you dearly. And to my children—Adrian, Katrina, and Alexandria—your love, compassion, generosity, success in life and as parents, and your support for me and honest feedback about just about everything is a true miracle, given how much of a basket case I was when you were sick as kids. The beautiful partners you've chosen and those seven grandchildren you've given us are the greatest gifts a mother could ask for. And Creba: thank you for throwing up in my car when you were four. It was the final frontier.

To my intelligent, friendly, and funny writing partner, David Russ, whom I have never even met in person. You are an amazing psychologist and I have learned so much from you through this writing process. So many children who had emetophobia and were under your care are more fortunate than they will ever realize.

We are both greatly indebted to all those scholars who have researched emetophobia and to the authors who have written about it most recently: Alexandra Keyes, David Veale, Dara Lovitz, David Yusko, and Ken Goodman. Finally, thank you to the great people at Jessica Kingsley who took a chance on us as new authors and this important book.

## Dr David Russ

I have to thank my daughter who made me realize that something had to be done to help. I am still sad she had to go through such anxiety, but now she is a happy, wonderful person and wife I can look back and see the good it set in motion. Professionally, it led to one of the most satisfying forks in the road I could have ever taken.

My sweet wife, Linda, has been my steadfast supporter throughout this project (and life). I just had to mention "book" and she would do whatever she could to help me. What father specializes in vomit? I have enjoyed the good-hearted teasing from my kids. Once while taking a picture of throw up (clandestinely by the way), they said, "Dad, what are you doing?! What father does that?" I still laugh thinking of the playful exchange. Thank you, God, for my wife and kids.

Many years ago now, I took a gamble and contacted the most famous emetophobia treatment provider in the world and asked her if she wanted to write a book. To my shock, Anna said yes. Virtually every clinician in the English-speaking world who treats this has used her site. It has been my rich privilege to co-author with her. The things her experience has taught her... wow. I get to "borrow" even more stuff from her.

I am a simple guy. It gives me the greatest joy to make a kid laugh at my silly jokes while watching them beat this fear. Thank you to all my patients who trusted me to help them... and sometimes laughed. I don't care if you faked it.

Jane and Maudisa, thank you for thinking this idea was relevant, needed, and worth publishing! You have been amazing to work with.

# Disclaimers

Anyone using this book for self-help is advised to consult with a physician or licensed mental health provider before use as you may require medical attention or diagnosis. The information contained in this book is not intended to replace the services of trained medical professionals or to be a substitute for medical advice.

Case studies throughout the book use pseudonyms, and may be amalgamations of multiple real cases.

## Content Warning

Words used and concepts discussed in this book may be upsetting to people with emetophobia.

# Foreword

At one level emetophobia shares many of the features of other anxiety disorders. There is intolerance of uncertainty, an over-estimation of the threat and awfulness of vomiting, and attentional biases towards the threat of vomiting. There is marked avoidance and safety-seeking behaviors, and often repeated checking and reassurance seeking. However, there are also several differences in emetophobia. For example, why does emetophobia have an increased female bias compared to other specific phobias? Is emetophobia best conceptualized as a type of obsessive-compulsive disorder? Why do people with emetophobia often have disordered eating? Why is emetophobia not treated seriously by some clinicians? Do you have to repeatedly vomit to confront your fear? Why is emetophobia so tricky to treat compared to other specific phobias? The internet is riddled with claims of cure by untested therapies. The reality is that even the gold standard treatment of cognitive behavior therapy that includes exposure may only help about two-thirds of sufferers. It does not necessarily cure them but may significantly improve their quality of life and shift them from a phobia of vomiting to a fear of vomiting. Much research is required to improve outcomes. Anna Christie and David Russ provide a masterclass in helping us to understand what we know and how to treat emetophobia. I hope it will stimulate you to research emetophobia and to improve your practice.

*Dr David Veale*
*Consultant Psychiatrist, South London and Maudsley NHS*
*Foundation Trust, Visiting Professor, Institute of Psychiatry,*
*Psychology and Neurosciences, Kings College London,*
*and author of* Free Yourself from Emetophobia

# Preface

## ANNA'S STORY—PART 1

They say my father was never the same after my brother died. Of course. What would one expect? But he was still my dad, my everything, my rock, my whole world. Kenny was 17 when he died, my sister was 15, and I was just three years old. I remember about a year after Kenny's accident I thought it might be fun to swallow a Bermuda penny—a little bigger than a quarter. The penny got stuck in my throat, and through some miracle of the universe, it didn't block my airway. I told my sister who was babysitting me at the time, and she ran next door and got the neighbor who was a nurse.

"We have to make you vomit," the nurse said. She mixed up some mustard powder with salt and warm water. It's a wonder she didn't kill me with this idea, but anyway, I still have a picture in my mind of standing with the two of them over a toilet but not vomiting. Then the nurse stuck her finger down my throat, and I still didn't vomit, but I was totally not impressed.

When my parents got home, they rushed me to the hospital, and I recall being wheeled down the hallway and freaking out that I had to leave my dad. As an adult and psychotherapist, I can reflect on this experience now and conclude that my father had become my primary attachment figure. Let's sum that up by just saying that my mom would never have received a "mother of the year" award. She once told my dad that she hated children and only had them because he wanted them.

I guess that the penny-swallowing episode was a traumatic event for a four-year-old. I don't really know. I have a clear memory of it, but again that alone does not account for a phobia because a lot of kids go through emergency surgery and all manner of medical procedures, and they don't have phobias, let alone emetophobia. I do know that from around that time, or perhaps earlier after Kenny died, I became terrified of people lying down. When Kenny was in the hospital and in an iron lung with a traumatic brain injury, my parents just told me he was "sick." "Very, very sick." He died five days later. After that, if someone was lying on their couch or in bed, I would not go into the room. My mother tells the story of a time when I was a preschooler, and we went to a family gathering. My uncle Blondie was lying on his couch watching the hockey game. I came around the corner to see him and immediately started crying and clinging to my dad. "Blondie, would you mind sitting up?" dad asked.

"Sure," he said. He sat up, and I was perfectly fine.

I remember the next few years being afraid of sickness, sick people, people in bed/lying down, or feeling sick myself. I don't think I would have been diagnosed with emetophobia just yet. But then my dad, the center of my world, got colon cancer.

## Chapter 1

# UNDERSTANDING EMETOPHOBIA

It is a great relief that, finally, in the early 2020s, respectable books are being published to help people with emetophobia (see Appendix 1 for a list of resources). Emetophobia is one of the most debilitating anxiety disorders with the least amount of research or help available. Happily, that seems to be changing. What was still missing was a book for clinicians that included the substantial research base for treating anxiety disorders but was fine-tuned by the thousands of clinical hours we have between us in treating emetophobia in adults and children. Emetophobia is like other phobias in many ways but, as you may be aware if you have tried to treat it, it has some significant and unique features. We note research throughout this book where it is relevant and also provide a complete list, in chronological order, of all research on emetophobia to date in Appendix 2. Only 73 studies have been done, most of them single case studies, and several of these are in languages other than English.

## What Is Emetophobia?

Emetophobia, or the specific fear of vomiting (SPOV), is categorized by the American Psychiatric Association in the DSM-5-TR (2022, pp. 224–229) under the umbrella of anxiety disorders. Within that broad category, it is in the sub-category of phobias and listed as "other." The classic categories are phobias associated with animals, environments, blood-injection-injury, situations, and the catch-all "other" type with the parenthetical example "situations that may lead to choking or vomiting." The correct DSM-5-TR code for emetophobia is therefore F40.298.

To meet the standard of a phobia, the reaction must be intense or severe, and this could happen when in the actual presence of or in anticipation of the stimulus. The reaction can range from high anxiety to a panic attack. Additionally, this reaction is elicited nearly every time the stimulus is present. As a result, anything associated with the subject of the fear is actively avoided. The desire to avoid can be extraordinary and significantly interfere with daily life. The force of symptoms causes significant distress in school, work, social, and other areas. Also, the reaction must be clearly out of proportion (to an objective observer) to the actual danger that the object or situation poses. In the case of emetophobia, patients may recognize that their response is extreme; others may believe their interpretation of the threat is accurate. Whether the patient is aware that their interpretation of the threat is accurate or not has little impact on diagnosis but a significant impact on treatment. Lastly, the anxiety or fear and the behavioral avoidance are stubbornly persistent. The diagnostic criteria state the symptoms must be present for at least six months to rule out a transient episode. Nevertheless, we have treated and diagnosed patients who clearly have emetophobia that is not transient, and it has been present for less than six months. This may particularly be the case with children if school refusal is one of the avoidance symptoms.

This fear centers around anything that may lead to vomiting or any nausea-invoking activities or situations. Most people with emetophobia fear vomiting themselves, while a smaller percentage only fear seeing and/or hearing someone else vomit. Anna, and only a handful of others we've come across, belong to the second type. However, after a few hundred hours of her own work, she is now of the opinion that the phobia began as a fear of vomiting herself and that this characteristic still lay beneath the surface.

People with emetophobia who only fear vomiting themselves usually fear others vomiting if they have something contagious. Some people with emetophobia do not experience raised anxiety when looking at photos or even videos of people who are drunk, pregnant, or trying the "gallon of milk challenge." If the person doesn't look sick, they don't get anxious. On the other hand, some people with emetophobia are so terrified that they don't give anyone vomiting the benefit of the doubt in case, for example, they're pregnant *and* they have norovirus[1] or something else that might be contagious.

Keyes, Gilpin, and Veale (2018) noted that another aspect of the fear is vomiting in public and the imagined subsequent shame. Boschen (2007) proposes that people with emetophobia may have an exaggerated sense of how negatively others would interpret their vomiting. Perhaps they believe observers might view someone getting sick as weakness or react with extreme disgust. The imagined negative evaluation is catastrophic, and the judgment and embarrassment are considered unbearable. In one study by Van Hout and Bouman (2011), the fear of oneself vomiting was endorsed by 77 percent, vomiting in front of others was about 40 percent, 45 percent seeing someone else vomit, and 21 percent a combination of all three. The relative intensity of the various loci of the fear was not apparent in the survey.

One of David's adult patients reported that her great fear was to vomit in a social situation, have it recorded on a device, and then published on a social media platform. The example she gave was imagining she was in a wedding party during the ceremony (this would almost certainly be filmed in its entirety) and at some point throwing up, upsetting the ceremony, irritating the bride and groom, and, to top it off, have it streamed online.

Further recognizing the social aspect of the phobia, a survey of adults by Lipsitz et al. (2001), noted that two-thirds of the respondents reported being more afraid to vomit in public than in private. In our experience with children (ages 6–11) with emetophobia, increased fear of vomiting in public is comparatively rare.

## Etiology

Lipsitz et al. (2001) noted that only about 30 percent of respondents recalled severe and/or vivid vomiting incidents. Almost 60 percent reported vividly remembering other people vomiting. About 20 percent had significant childhood medical incidents, some of which involved vomiting, and 57 percent had a first-degree relative diagnosed with a psychiatric disorder. Veale (2009, p. 277) notes that "it may be

---

1    Norovirus is the name given to all "Norwalk-like viruses" or what many refer to as "stomach flu" (a misnomer as the virus is not influenza), "stomach bug," "winter vomiting virus," or "viral gastroenteritis."

difficult to identify any associations or meaning of vomiting from very early experiences and the only association is that of overwhelming fear."

Considering the origins of the phobia, Veale et al. (2013b) proposed possible pathways that could result in a phobia. They suggest, as have many others, that the phobia is a consequence of associated experiences. The person has an aversive experience that creates the conditions that actuate the phobia, or observes it happening to someone else and acquires it vicariously.

## ANNA'S STORY—PART 2

The first symptom of colon cancer that my dad had was a lot of vomiting. I remember being terrified of that sound. By this time, I was eight years old, and because it was 1967, nobody thought it was a good idea to tell children the truth about what was happening to their parent when they were dying. So, dad's death a year later came as a terrible shock—to me—but not to anyone else. My sister was married and had moved away, and I was left in this world with only my rather mean, angry mother. By this time, I had full-blown emetophobia.

Another etiological theory noted by Veale et al. (2013b) is that the phobia develops apart from any specific experience. The fear may be acquired through "evolution and innate pathways" (p. 13) that identify danger. They propose that this second pathway is not as likely since vomiting is biologically advantageous. The researchers also observe the comorbidity between SPOV and other anxiety disorders, suggesting a factor is a heightened anxiety vulnerability that increases the chance of developing a disorder. Associated with this vulnerability is the tendency to misinterpret body sensations catastrophically. If this is coupled with hypervigilance to these sensations, then avoidance and negative beliefs lead to the formation of the phobia.

In the same article, Veale et al. (2013b) report that, compared to a control group, participants with SPOV experienced memories of vomiting as more distressing and the consequences more aversive. Before the onset of the phobia, there were no differences in the number of memories of themselves vomiting recalled by either group. However, after the onset of the phobia, the number of memories of them vomiting was less for the SPOV group, but the recollection of other people vomiting was higher. This suggests that the SPOV group is likely avoiding and using safety behaviors with some success but at a cost to the quality of their lives. Additionally, the increased recollections of others' vomiting may be due to it happening more around them, but is more likely a bias resulting from "selective attention and hypervigilance" (p. 18) to the perceived threat. They note it supports Rachman's (1977) vicarious learning theory.

The SPOV group reported more aversive surrounding aspects of the memories as well. Some examples they gave were: vomiting was unpredictable, the cause was more upsetting, and a parent provided no comfort. In other words, the context of the events may play a vital role in the anxiety. Following Ehlers and Clark (2000), they theorize that distressing memories may be subject to a similar process that happens in post-traumatic stress disorder (PTSD). The memory/experience is biased by an excessively negative appraisal of the event and/or related events. The autobiographical component is characterized by incomplete/inconsistent recall and loss of context. These memories may be experienced as flashbacks or flash-forwards. The moments of distress may be experienced without a time perspective and/or context. The fear and physical distress may be like that experienced at the time of the original vomiting experience. In other words, the composition of memories creates a sense of a serious current threat.

In a study by Price, Veale, and Brewin (2012), 80 percent of adult subjects reported, when anxious, intrusive imagery about vomiting. These included childhood memories, adult memories, and imagined "flash-forwards" to catastrophic scenarios. Interestingly, the imagined future scenarios often dramatically exaggerate both the amount and length of time of vomiting. (In our experience, this same distortion may also be present in memories.) The imagery always contained some visual features but also had elements of physical sensations, vomiting sounds, reactions of others, tastes, and smells. Aversive memories or amalgamations probably account for more of the intrusive imagery than constructed future scenarios. Some of the most anxious participants had relatively little imagery because of a focus on physical sensations, concentration on not getting sick, and use of safety behaviors.

Based on a sample of Salvadorian youths, Wu et al. (2016) found that those with emetophobic symptoms correlated with higher externalizing symptoms. They theorized that coupled with anxiety sensitivity and the accompanying intolerance to anxiety, provoking stimuli could potentially result in "emotionally dysregulated reactions" to vomit-associated situations. They also observed increased obsessive-compulsive disorder (OCD) symptoms, particularly checking, doubting, and neutralizing compulsions.

Boschen (2007) proposed that emetophobia may have seven components in three phases. In the first phase, "predisposing factors," there is an inherited vulnerability to anxiety in general and a vulnerability to somaticize anxiety symptoms. In the second, the "acute phase," he proposes there could be catastrophic misappraisal, accompanying hypervigilance, as well as thoughts/beliefs about the meaning and shame of vomiting. In the third "maintenance phase," there is the avoidance of nausea and/or potential triggers leading to the failure to habituate and missed opportunities to learn from behavior and experiences that would disconfirm the threat.

Boschen (2007) also proposes different feedback loops contributing to the phobia. The first is when the phobic person may perceive they are sick, which leads to an escalation of gastrointestinal somatic symptoms. An additional feedback loop is worry about future vomiting. This vigilance leads to noticing any interoceptive cues of gastric distress. This, plus the occurrence of normal digestive processes, may elicit a catastrophic interpretation of those cues. Another loop is avoiding any stimuli that could cause nausea. The result is the failure to habituate to gastric sensations and a reduction of self-efficacy.

Using results from research with SPOV participants, Verwoerd, Van Hout, and De Jong (2016) observed that the subjects strongly relied on emotional reasoning to validate dysfunctional cognitions. If someone *feels* anxious, they *believe* it is accurately signaling danger. Also, rather than only measuring feelings of anxiety, they measured feelings of disgust. They found that feelings of disgust primarily drove the high vomit-anxiety group.

Cili and Stopa (2015) propose that intrusive mental imagery may contribute to or maintain any disorder. They describe the imagery as vivid, possibly with other sensory modalities. The images are often recurrent and triggered by specific stimuli. The researchers note that in the case of emetophobia, stomach sensations or seeing another person who looks unwell can trigger intrusive images. The images may be related or recalled from past experiences. Some may be compiled or adapted to be more products of one's imagination rather than actual experiences. In our understanding, these images or sensory elements are virtually universal in people with emetophobia.

Our combined clinical experience with over 300 patients with emetophobia has demonstrated that there seems to be no single cause but rather a "perfect storm" of several factors in childhood. Not all our patients have experienced trauma. We have also observed a disturbance in the normal secure attachment with the mother at a young age. Sometimes this takes the form of the mother not being very warm, especially when a child is sick, but at other times the mother has simply gone back to work. One child I (Anna) worked with got norovirus when, obviously through no fault of her own, her mother was in the hospital giving birth to their sister and the child was staying with grandma. Despite a truly lovely family situation, this child experienced regular separation anxiety after that, along with emetophobia. We tell our patients that no matter what the cause of their emetophobia the treatment is the same, so, as is normal with the CBT protocol, we do not spend excessive time with patients trying to determine a cause.

## Prevalence

According to Philips (1985), Kirkpatrick and Berg (1981) conducted an analytic study of fears of a heterogenous nonpsychiatric sample. They found that "vomiting fears are present at the 'extreme or terror' level for 3.1% of males and 6% of females" (Philips 1985, p. 45).

Lipsitz et al. (2001) found this phobia to be more common in women with an average duration of 22 years at the time they were interviewed. Only 12 percent reported remission of symptoms for longer than six months. Over 90 percent reported distress from symptoms 52 weeks a year. Over 70 percent said they were distressed six to seven days per week. The average age of onset was 9.2 years. Veale and Lambrou (2006) report the mean age of onset as 9.8 years.

With a sample of 547 students, Kartsounis, Mervyn-Smith, and Pickersgill (1983) ranked the fear of nausea 16th out of 88. A Dutch self-report survey by Van Hout and Bouman (2011) found the community prevalence at 8.8 percent, with a ratio of 4:1 female to male. Becker et al. (2007) reported that emetophobia is rare (0.1%) compared to other specific phobias. Research on a sample of Salvadoran youths by Wu et al. (2016) reported elevated emetophobic symptoms in 7.5 percent of participants. Unlike earlier studies, they did not find a gender difference.

Keyes, Gilpin, and Veale (2018) note that community rates may be lower than what clinicians encounter, suggesting higher prevalence in clinical samples. A range of .1 percent to 8.8 percent is hardly conclusive and is likely a result of methodological differences in collecting the data. Nevertheless, although the prevalence is not clear and likely underestimated in the literature, this phobia impacts literally millions of children and adults globally.

## Characteristics
### Severity
Emetophobia presents as extreme fear and subsequent distress. Commonly, a person with emetophobia will experience debilitating anxiety or a panic attack. They nearly all describe having panic attacks that last for several hours, even though research on anxiety suggests that a panic attack only lasts a few minutes. I (Anna) remember that if the perceived threat were present (either nausea or the presence of a nauseous person), then the panic feeling would persist. Emetophobia may also produce more chronic anxiety which can either slowly rise to panic levels or instantaneously surge. This is often precipitated by a body sensation (e.g., stomach ache).

The panic response can include any of the following: rapid heartbeat, the rush of adrenalin, difficulty breathing, choking or gagging sensations, derealization, dizziness, fear of dying, numbness in extremities, hot flush, and sweating. If derealization is strong, the person with emetophobia experiences what is akin to a PTSD flashback which can be accompanied by screaming, fighting, throwing, breaking things, or running indiscriminately, sometimes even into the path of actual danger. We notice these last symptoms especially, but not exclusively, in children. It is important to note here that the clinical presentation of emetophobia is almost universally this severe, although most patients present as stable, intelligent, psychologically healthy people when not triggered.

Many people with emetophobia report quite sincerely that they would rather die than vomit. For many, vomiting and death anxiety are inextricably linked. Veale (2009) notes that vomiting may feel like suffocation or even death. These aversive experiences can be associated with various stimuli and are highly durable. The activating stimuli are automatic and "relatively impenetrable" to reasoning. People with emetophobia cannot reason their way out of the fear, so family members' or clinicians' insistence on logic and reason is similarly futile.

Catastrophizing is commonly used by researchers and clinicians to describe the tendency to amplify a possible threat and to magnify the likely consequences. Gellatly and Beck (2016) propose that this cognitive process is transdiagnostic because it is part of virtually every type of anxiety or related disorder. Specifically, they describe the process of catastrophizing, when it is about a health concern, as a tendency to view bodily symptoms as nearly always disastrous. Patients overestimate the likelihood they have the feared condition, believe symptoms to be extremely serious, and interpret physical or psychological sensations as signs of the feared health issue. In a study by Veale and Lambrou (2006), people with emetophobia rated statements about the awfulness of vomiting, losing control, becoming ill, and others finding them repulsive even higher than a panic disorder group. They also rated these concerns as having a high probability of occurring.

## ANNA'S STORY—PART 3

In August of 1996, my family drove from Vancouver to Los Angeles so my 13-year-old daughter could perform with her dance school in Disneyland. Although flying would have been simpler, I convinced my husband that we should drive and make a fun road trip out of it. In reality, I was too afraid to fly in case someone on the plane vomited near me as there was no way to "escape." Nothing could have prepared me for what happened on that trip.

The drive down was uneventful, as was Disneyland. But on the way back, we took the scenic route, which was a windy road along the coast. I was driving, and my two daughters were in the back row of our minivan. Suddenly I heard coughing and asked, "What's that?" It was my 11-year-old, vomiting. "OH NO!" I screamed. My worst nightmare was being in a car with someone who got carsick. Or anywhere "trapped" while someone is vomiting.

"It's in the garbage can!" yelled my 13-year-old, as if that would make it okay.

I brought the car to a screeching stop on a very narrow shoulder, jumped out, and ran halfway up a cliff, blinded to reality, my heart pounding. I was crying uncontrollably and gasping for air. I sat down with my head in my hands, shaking with adrenalin and sobbing. My husband sat down beside me and tried to console me. "She's okay now. It's okay."

It was not okay. Nothing about this was okay. Suddenly I found myself saying through the sobs, "I want my dad. I want my dad." I was 36 years old, and my dad died when I was nine. Even as I was repeating these words over and over again out loud, I could not figure out why I was doing it. I felt silly saying them, but at first, nothing else would come out of my mouth.

My husband tried to get me back in the car, but there was no way in hell I would do that. I was frozen there on that California cliff, paralyzed with fear. All that went through my head was how to get home from northern California to Vancouver without flying, getting on a bus, or getting back in my car. Once I could say something other than "I want my dad," I just began insisting that I would not get back in the car and that my husband should just drive home and leave me there on the cliff, over 1000 kilometers from home.

Eventually, my legs worked. I opened the sliding door of the van, and my 11-year-old was crying and apologized and said she was fine now: the road had just been too windy. I remember telling her, "It's not your fault. I just have this terrible fear, and I don't know why, but it is absolutely not your fault, okay?" She nodded. Luckily, she never got emetophobia herself and seems to be very well-adjusted now as a wife and mother of two, with two college degrees and a career.

We drove a few miles to a town and rented an expensive two-bedroom, two-bathroom suite in a hotel. It was perfect for me to be able to calm down. I also had two Valium with me, so I took a hot bath and took one and went to sleep. The next day we headed out for the main highway: no more scenic route. I took the other Valium and somehow made it home in that car.

---

As clinicians, you must know that, for those with emetophobia, anything related to vomiting has the potential to cause panic like this. Many of our patients experience a mind-numbing, gripping terror when they feel just a little full, gassy, or queasy. For that reason, you must approach this clinically in a gentle and cautious manner until you have established rapport, educated yourself and your patient, and developed a plan.

Even the standard practice of gathering a history may potentially elicit a great deal of anxiety. If someone is sitting in your office, they are desperate, courageous, and terrified. Desperate because this fear is so debilitating. Courageous because the very act of coming for help is threatening. Terrified because they know they will need to talk about and potentially face the very thing that is so horrifying they will do nearly anything to escape it.

## Control

In the 1970s and 1980s, the concept of locus (location) of control (LOC) was quite prominent. Those with primarily *internal* LOC regard events in their lives as being within their influence. They believe they can affect the events around them. Those with primarily *external* LOC think that events in their lives are outside their control or that their ability to influence such events is negligible. Typically, anxiety and depression are associated with having an external LOC. Davidson, Boyle, and Lauchlan (2007) demonstrated that people with emetophobia had a significantly higher internal LOC. They believe that, with enough effort, they can prevent themselves from vomiting. Assuming the findings from this study are generalizable, clinicians encouraging their patients to give up this control with the attending safety and coping mechanisms and/or insisting that the patient does not have any control over vomiting should expect quite a bit of resistance.

One cannot control vomiting, just as one cannot control diarrhea, but adults do have a warning about both, which is why you don't see adults vomiting or exploding in their pants unless they're intoxicated. We do have time to make it to the nearest bathroom or receptacle. We believe that since emetophobia begins in childhood, when children have little to no warning of vomiting or do not recognize the signs, the adult with emetophobia assumes the same. We have had many patients tell us, "It's been so long since I've vomited that I'm afraid I won't know how and won't recognize the signs," or, "Because I'm nauseous all the time, but it's just anxiety, I'm afraid I won't recognize the real thing." Neither of these worries is based in reality, and this is one time (and only one) when we don't refrain from reassuring our patients: "It's different. You will know." If you try to explain *how* they will know, they may either begin imagining that symptom all the time or actually develop it.

## Intolerance of Uncertainty or Risk

The intolerance of uncertainty for whatever is feared is a salient feature of anxiety disorders. When there is no significant anxiety, the assumption is that "it" is safe unless proven dangerous. With anxiety, the assumption is that "it" is dangerous unless proven safe (virtually impossible). People with emetophobia cannot tolerate the uncertainty of not knowing when they might vomit and will not risk it. However, most people with emetophobia will get into a car with no thought of their safety, even though the risk of dying in a car accident is 1 in 101 (National Safety Council 2022) while the risk of dying while vomiting is exactly zero, so long as one is not unconscious. We have had more than one patient terrified of vomiting in public if they went out of the house after eating or being too full. The odds of an adult vomiting in public are infinitesimally small. And yet more than one patient has told us that even if there is a 0.0000000001 percent chance that it might happen, it is too great of a risk.

## Nausea

A prominent feature of emetophobia is the presence or feared onset of nausea. In a survey of a group of people with emetophobia by Höller et al. (2013), researchers found that just over 80 percent of subjects suffered from nausea. Of that group, 77 percent had intermittent breaks from nausea, and 23 percent reported unremitting distress. The duration ranged from less than 30 minutes to four hours or longer. For 65 percent of participants, nausea interfered with their routine duties. Almost half described nausea as so intense they believed they were going to vomit. However, 98 percent reported they did not vomit when they were nauseated.

Although gastrointestinal distress is associated with many anxiety disorders, it is a primary component in the experience of those with emetophobia. For example, in one survey by Veale and Lambrou (2006), participants with emetophobia reported significantly more frequent and longer nausea episodes than those with panic disorder.

In our experience, this is a bit of a chicken and egg phenomenon. Nausea may trigger anxiety or be a result of anxiety. Most people with emetophobia are so hypervigilant to any possible gastrointestinal discomfort that they may interpret it catastrophically, ironically causing the distress to worsen. For some, even minor discomfort can lead to increasing distress creating a vicious cycle. It is easy to imagine that attempting to avoid nausea is typical of the disorder. On the other hand, there may be an underlying biological condition that needs treatment. This is discussed at length in Chapter 3.

We encourage our patients, if they have not already done so, to explore all medical possibilities for chronic or recurring nausea, preferably with a gastroenterologist. This exploration may include imaging, endoscopy, colonoscopy, esophagogram, etc. Many people with emetophobia will be too afraid to undergo such tests if the preparation or the tests themselves cause them to vomit. Frequently, children we see will have already had testing as they don't usually have a choice, and have additionally undergone dietary changes or restrictions. Sometimes the only way to determine the cause of the nausea is for the patient to have undergone treatment for their anxiety disorder to see if nausea remains when the anxiety is significantly reduced or gone.

### Eating Behavior

Characteristic of any anxiety disorder is the attempt to remove the threat. Food restriction or selective eating is typical with emetophobia. If the result is being underweight, it can appear like an eating disorder but be very different in the underlying reasons, beliefs, and assumptions.

Veale et al. (2012) identify three ways people with emetophobia may restrict food:

1. The amount eaten is restricted. Often the desired outcome is to remain hungry or more likely avoid the feeling of being "full."
2. Food is restricted in specific contexts such as in restaurants or cooked by someone else.
3. Types of food are restricted. This may include food that has been interpreted but not experienced as "dangerous." People with emetophobia may have heard that certain foods are at higher risk for food poisoning, for example.

In this same study (Veale et al. 2012), restricted eating among those diagnosed with emetophobia resulted in more severe symptoms and impairment. It was hypothesized, for example, that food restriction led to increased feelings of nausea which in turn led to misinterpreting those feelings as increasing the threat of vomiting. Food restriction was likely interpreted as reducing the possibility of vomiting, resulting in a sense of control, all of which is reinforcing. It was evident in this study that restricting food was to reduce the threat of vomiting and not for body or weight concerns.

### Avoidance and Safety Behaviors

Chief among the characteristics and behavior of people with emetophobia is the fierce and persistent desire to avoid anything connected to vomiting. Since that is virtually impossible, as with all anxiety disorders, secondary avoidance or safety behaviors become the following line of defense. Common safety behaviors include checking expiration dates, sipping on water, and excessive use of antacids, ginger, peppermints, etc. These safety behaviors may also occur in the patient's mind, where they convince themselves that they won't be sick with all sorts of interesting and creative mental games. They may even employ superstitions unbeknownst to the clinician.

Given the early onset of emetophobia, avoidance of vomiting becomes somewhat "natural" as, especially when we become adults, we only vomit on average once every 10–20 years. This, inadvertently, leads to the false assumption that all the avoiding and safety behaviors have been effective. Unfortunately, the opposite happens: these behaviors perpetuate and exacerbate the phobia.

In a systematic review, Keyes, Gilpin, and Veale (2018) reported seven studies examining avoidance behaviors. Four studies focused on avoiding people or situations. Three focused on avoiding food. They also noted six papers that examined safety-seeking behaviors such as checking expiration dates on food, eating rituals, and self and other monitoring for well-being. Even though the previous list is quite extensive, we are ever surprised by the creativity and resourcefulness of patients' attempts to avoid vomiting or make situations "safer."

Clinicians should be aware and frequently check with their patients about what they are doing. Often the safety behaviors can be quite subtle. For example, I (David) was working with a young patient via video and during exposures, off-camera, he was flicking his fingers. This was his way of "flicking away" the triggering image we were practicing. It is also not uncommon to hear a patient neutralize a picture of someone who looks unwell by imagining it won't lead to vomiting or a picture of someone vomiting as not sick but drunk, which isn't contagious. These behaviors will be discussed at length throughout the book.

## Symptom and Behavior List

The following is a comprehensive but not exhaustive list of some of the most common symptoms and behaviors exhibited by patients with emetophobia. As you review them, some may appear to be opposites. It all depends on what has become associated with the phobia. The fundamental principle behind every symptom or behavior is that the activating fear is always about vomiting.

### Fear of Others

- Sick or injured people no matter what condition, as vomiting can be a symptom of numerous illnesses.
- Children (as they vomit more often, sometimes without warning, and they are more prone to viruses).
- Others burping, holding their stomachs, looking pallid, coughing, bending at the waist, standing by a car on the side of the road, or saying they don't feel well.
- People who have been sick, their personal items, and areas of contact (e.g., school desk); houses where others have been sick in the previous days to weeks.
- Vomiting in front of other people.
- Animals that vomit.

### Fear of Situations and Things

- Anything that may be contaminated by a virus, e.g., items, furniture, clothing, rooms, etc.
- Public toilets (someone may enter and vomit or will have already vomited there).
- Eating out or eating food one has not prepared (in case it may lead to food poisoning, which would cause vomiting).

- Bedtime or nightfall (as they may have memories of being sick in the night as a child), sleeping alone, and/or nightmares about vomiting.
- Seeing vomiting on television, in movies, or in books (vomiting is commonplace in the media).
- Traveling by plane, boat, train, public transportation, or auto (in case they or someone else are motion sick and it may be difficult or impossible to exit).
- Performance situations that might elicit vomiting (as they will have heard of others vomiting from nerves).
- Psychotherapy (lest it involves talking about vomit or exposure therapy which they feel they can't handle or misunderstand to mean they must vomit).
- Hospitals, medical/dental offices, procedures, and nursing facilities.
- Amusement parks where people may be sick on rides.
- Going to school or other public places.
- Fall and winter because of the likely increase in cases of norovirus.
- Pregnancy (due to morning sickness or vomiting during delivery).
- Highly disgusting smells and/or sights.
- Several kinds of job.

## Fear of Consumption

- Food and/or drink associated with vomiting (past, self, others, news of food poisoning).
- Feeling full.
- Possibility of choking and then vomiting.
- Taking any prescription medication that may have nausea or vomiting as a listed side-effect (which is virtually all, even anti-emetics).
- Anesthesia due to vomiting as a side-effect.
- Alcohol consumption, or events where alcohol is consumed.

## Fear of Interoception

- Feeling nauseous, gassy, bloated, crampy, queasy, hungry, churning, or having diarrhea or loose stool.
- Tightness or lump in the throat.
- Feeling dizziness, headache, feverish, achy.
- Feeling hot or ambient temperature too warm.

## Reactivity

When triggered (which is daily in almost all people with emetophobia), anxiety ranges from extreme fear to full panic attacks.

- Dissociation, inability to reason, crying, screaming, pacing, begging for help.
- Non-suicidal self-injury in the form of scratching skin, hair-pulling, cutting, feigned "suicide" attempts.
- Harming others, or property.
- Strong feelings of anger, frustration, shame, guilt, and despair at not being believed, understood, or supported.

## Safety Behaviors

Checking

- Hypervigilance and scanning a crowd or group for people who look unwell.
- Constant body scanning/ruminating about how they feel.
- Checking their temperature or asking a parent or teacher to check it.
- Asking for frequent reassurance, "Do you think I will get sick?"
- Checking on how other people are feeling.
- Checking expiration dates on food (not just refrigerated foods, anything with a date on it) and throwing it out or asking about how long something has been out of the refrigerator.
- Scanning for bathrooms and exits, sitting in places only near exits.
- Checking that food is fully cooked, overcooking food.
- Checking online for news on norovirus outbreaks, the meaning of symptoms, causes of nausea and vomiting, etc.

Avoiding

- Talking about vomit or saying the word.
- Being alone and insisting on being with a "safe person" or avoiding being with anyone else.
- Sleeping away from home.
- Remaining near a sick person even if it is their child or a family member who needs their help (this can result in enormous guilt).
- Relationships because someone was ill or could be sick.
- Going into a bathroom or fetching a bowl/bucket (as it may "make them vomit").
- Hearing someone vomit (plugging ears).
- Getting pregnant and possibly sexual activity.
- Eating or drinking, or eating very little.
- Specific foods except what they have deemed safe (some reasons include texture, contains raw egg, might cause burping, associated with vomiting).
- Eating leftovers even if refrigerated or known to be safe.
- Medical help (in case they are trapped in a hospital with more sick people).
- Medication (in case the side effects are nausea/vomiting).
- Places, situations, or crowds (where one could vomit, see vomit or someone vomiting, or hear someone had vomited there).
- Eating at normal speed (which they deem "too quickly").
- Eating with anyone else.
- Eating food when the preparation cannot be controlled or observed (restaurants, friends' or family's home).
- Touching things that might be contaminated with germs (norovirus) like knobs, buttons, surfaces, items in the grocery store, money, etc.
- School, riding the bus, participating in gym.
- Visual or physical motion sickness causing activities (e.g., 3D movies, boats, trains, rides, etc.).
- Wearing clothing worn when sick, or fabrics of the same color.
- Specific time commitments because unable to predict how one will be feeling.
- Anxiety-provoking situations in general.

## Prevention

- Use of over-the-counter medications to control vomiting (Pepto Bismol, Dramamine, Tums, Gas-X, etc.).
- Prescription anti-emetic medication or tranquilizers.
- Chewing gum or sucking on lozenges or mints, usually peppermint.
- Always carrying bottled water and sipping it when "nauseous".
- Taking a "safety kit" with them which may contain items such as medications, mints, water, and a plastic bag.
- Insisting on having a parent or grandparent sit in the classroom.
- Refusing to put children in daycare, nursery, preschool, or school.
- Mental neutralizing, replaying, replacing, reassuring, distracting, and avoiding (this can be quite similar to the symptoms of OCD).
- Subtle behaviors like repeated swallowing, verbal sounds, posture changes, spitting.
- Excessive decontaminating (e.g., handwashing, bleaching counters, etc.) may also result in high use of paper, soap, and other cleaners.
- Performing various rituals or superstitious behaviors.

Copies of this checklist to use with patients are available on our website[2] (or scan the QR code below with your phone's camera and click the link that appears). You are free to print, copy, and use them with your patients.

---

2   www.emetophobia.net/about-emetophobia/handouts

— *Chapter 2* —

# DIFFERENTIAL DIAGNOSIS

## Making a Correct Diagnosis

Emetophobia shares symptoms with a variety of other mental health conditions. There are some, like OCD, where a failure to differentiate symptoms may have only a modest impact on treatment. However, failure to distinguish from an eating disorder can have disastrous consequences.

There is a qualifier for most DSM diagnoses. A diagnosis is given if the symptoms match the description *unless there is another diagnosis that better explains the symptoms*. If a patient comes to you expressing a fear connected with vomiting, emetophobia is likely a better explanation. Veale (2009, p. 273) writes: "A SPOV is relatively easy to diagnose when the patient presents with a fear of vomiting." Veale goes on to consider the differential diagnosis, including six of the misdiagnoses we examine further below.

People can easily diagnose emetophobia themselves. They know they're afraid of vomiting or of seeing/hearing others vomit, they usually know it's not rational, and they know for sure that the fear is ruining their lives. A frequent problem that most patients and clinicians run into with emetophobia is not patients diagnosing it themselves; it's that clinicians disagree with them and diagnose something else.

In children, diagnosis may not be as straightforward. A complicating factor is that descriptive words like "throw up," "puke," or "vomit" are carefully avoided by the child, so parents and clinicians may be left to guess the cause of the anxiety.

While writing, we found this personal story by Annie Reneau

(2022) in an *Upworthy* article. They noticed their daughter showing signs of increased anxiety. She, uncharacteristically, started to resist doing things or going places and would panic if there was an attempt to persuade her. Her mother observed:

> If she heard someone we knew was sick, she'd immediately ask with a worried tone, "What kind of sick?" ... It was clear she was struggling with anxiety, and we tried a couple of different therapists. They each helped a little, at least to keep the spiral from getting worse. But we seemed to be missing something.

She noticed her daughter felt frequent nausea, asked about food being safe, checked to see if it was fully cooked, and started to refuse to eat certain things. After observing these and other changes, her mother writes:

> And so, we started piecing it together. "I've noticed that most of your anxiety seems to be centered around you worrying about throwing up," I said to her one day. "Does that sound accurate?" She flinched when I said "throwing up," but nodded "yes."

We wish that Annie's experience was uncommon; it is not. These are loving, observant parents who are sincerely trying to help their children. What they don't know is that this phobia, more than almost any other form of anxiety, is initially furtive and involuntarily disguised, coming to light with hints and misdirection. This is not the intention of any child; rather, this is the nature of the phobia.

Regardless of intensity, situation, or expressed content, the core fear is always directed toward vomiting. For example, some patients will exhibit fear of the dentist, so it would seem to make sense to diagnose them with typical dental phobia. However, what they exactly fear is that a dental procedure will make them gag and vomit. One young man I (Anna) worked with was in dire need of dental work. I encouraged him to let the dentist and the assistant know about his phobia so they could be understanding and helpful. Unfortunately, when he told the assistant he was afraid of vomiting, she responded with, "Oh don't worry. People vomit in here all the time." Needless to say, he left, and it took an additional three sessions of working with him before he would go back.

## An Unfamiliar Diagnosis

Specific Phobia—Other Type (choking, vomiting): F40.298.

The DSM-5-TR (American Psychiatric Association 2022) coding above includes emetophobia, or as it is referred to by researchers, "specific phobia of vomiting" (SPOV). Relegating emetophobia to this "other type" category in the DSM may be one of the primary reasons clinicians are unfamiliar with it. For the specific wording of these criteria please consult the DSM-5-TR (American Psychiatric Association 2022, pp. 224–229).

People with phobias of dogs, clowns, injections, and heights can usually just avoid them. But people with emetophobia cannot avoid their own bodies. While at times their anticipatory or acute anxiety is triggered, often they experience a low level of nausea almost every day, keeping them chronically in a state of anticipation, which is excruciating, and no way to live.

## Diagnostic Instruments

Veale et al. (2013a) and Boschen et al. (2013) developed and tested two measures to assess and standardize the diagnosis, nature, and severity of emetophobia. The SPOVI (Veale et al. 2013a) and the EmetQ-13 (Boschen et al. 2013) have both been found to be valid and reliable (Maack, Ebesutani, and Smitherman 2017). These inventories are reproduced in Appendix 3.

If clinicians administer these inventories, they can do an objective assessment pre- and post-treatment and, if desired, at six-month or 12-month follow-up.

## Gathering a Relevant History
### The Patient's Story

I cannot count the times I (Anna) went to a therapist for emetophobia only to be told they were not interested in hearing my story. "Let's just start with the present-day" they would say. As emetophobia almost always begins in childhood, often before the patient can even remember, it is best to hear their story. Allowing the patient to recount their journey with emetophobia also helps to gain their trust.

## ANNA'S STORY—PART 4

I don't recall much before that fateful night in October 1962, just a month before my fourth birthday. My brother, Kenny, took off on his motorbike to see a movie with a friend. There were no helmet laws in Bermuda, where the speed limit on the whole island was 35 km. Nevertheless, if your bike light stops working and it's after dark, another motorcycle can inadvertently come down a blind hill and knock you flying off your bike, smashing your head into a cliff. Such was the phone call my parents got that night. "Your son is in the hospital in a coma, in an iron lung." Brain surgery relieved the pressure, but Kenny was left in a vegetative state, unable to breathe on his own. Five days he lingered in hospital. I remember asking for him every day, and mother would say, "Kenny is in hospital. He's very, very sick." In Bermuda, "sick" was the same word that the British folks who lived there used for vomiting. Kenny was very sick, and after the fifth day, he died.

Perhaps my emetophobic fate was pretty much sealed that day, although no one really knows everything that contributes to this phobia. Other people lose their brothers and don't get emetophobia.

## Attachment

My (Anna's) learning of attachment theory came through self-directed study, paying particular attention to the large body of work of John Bowlby, James Robertson, Harry Harlow, Mary Ainsworth, and others. Babies and later children go through an attunement and attachment process that begins with 100 percent attachment to the mother, and ideally ends with the child reaching the age of maturity, flying free of the nest, and perhaps one day beginning a family of their own. We refer to this as the natural way of attachment beginning and ending or being "resolved." Some babies borne by surrogates or mothers surrendering them for adoption are given at birth to their adoptive parents who may be males or females, and thus an attachment is formed with one or both parents who assume primary care for the infant. If everything goes well for that child from birth onward, then attachments are formed and resolved with the adoptive parent, and the child will grow up anxiety-free. However there is still some evidence that the child's first attachment was formed in utero, and especially if coupled with other factors, this break in attachment at birth could be instrumental in contributing to anxiety later in life (Zimerman and Doan 2003). Very few of us go through this process unscathed. Very few mothers, fathers, and other significant attachment figures go through it unscathed either: kids act out, parents get upset with them, some "helicopter" parents don't let kids fail things on their own, teenagers and parents get angry with one another, and so on.

With my patients with emetophobia, during intake and diagnosis, I am interested in as much as they can tell me about the attachment process with their mothers (and later other attachment figures). Having had over 200 patients with emetophobia, I have not had one with a secure, resolved attachment.

Many patients indicate that their mother was not a warm individual, and so the attachment was never secure enough for the patient to venture out into the world without anxiety. This is not to blame mothers, but rather to point out that even in some very lovely, very "functional" families, the child did not experience that mother or anyone else as emotionally available to them, particularly when they were very young and vomiting. One example that demonstrates that the family is not to blame, but might still be responsible through no fault of their own, is the case of an eight-year-old with emetophobia whose mother was in the hospital having a baby when the child got norovirus. There were no other issues with this family, and the child did well after about ten sessions.

## Family Systems

As I (Anna) was first trained as a family therapist before my CBT training, I always take one session to do a comprehensive family history with my patients. This involves drawing a genogram wherein I note the following significant features:

- physical or mental illnesses (diagnosed)
- suspected mental illness, especially anxiety, addiction, or depression
- relationships between the patient and members of their nuclear family
- dates of significant deaths and cause of death
- marriages, divorces, children, cutoff of family members by others
- family secrets, stories, traumas (wars, etc.), or folklore.

I staple the genogram on the inside front cover of the patient's file and refer to it before sessions until I have memorized a clear picture of the family within which the patient exists.

## Misdiagnoses

In our experience, misdiagnosis of emetophobia is a striking problem in the medical and psychotherapeutic community. It can result in a patient feeling excessive embarrassment or shame, mistrusting all clinicians, and, most importantly, receiving incorrect treatment. Since so many of the functions and symptoms of anxiety overlap, it is easy to confuse emetophobia with something else.

Diagnosis is also complicated by an increased or perceived comorbidity with other anxiety disorders. In a survey by Van Hout and Bouman (2011), respondents with emetophobia reported significantly higher rates of separate psychiatric conditions than the control groups. Panic, agoraphobia, and social anxiety were the most common. It is important to note that these were self-reports and not confirmed formal diagnoses. The pervasive desire to understand, coupled with ready access to the internet, will likely lead patients and/or parents to draw attention to possible diagnoses that could easily lead a clinician down the proverbial rabbit hole of misdiagnosis.

In a more recent article by Sykes, Boschen, and Conlon (2016) using structured clinical diagnostic interviews, the findings also support higher comorbidity rates in people with emetophobia. However, the comorbidity rates were lower overall than in the self-report data studies. These participants had confirmed diagnoses of SPOV. Panic, OCD, generalized anxiety disorder, social anxiety, depression, and illness anxiety were all at high levels of comorbidity. The overlapping and co-occurring anxiety symptoms can not only confuse the diagnosis but can lead a clinician to consider that comorbid conditions may need to be part of the treatment plan.

I (David) remember, in retrospect, the first time I ran into symptoms that I now recognize as emetophobia. I had been a practicing psychologist for almost 20 years and had never heard of a phobia of vomiting. The patient experienced, as is often the case, panic at various times, so I was quite certain it should have been diagnosed as a panic disorder. While consulting with various experienced clinicians about the case, the possibility of emetophobia never came up. The subject of fear of vomit arose as an aspect of the case, but none of us considered that as the principal problem. Panic attacks are so dramatic they naturally capture the patient's and clinician's attention.

As emetophobia has unique characteristics, it must receive specific treatment and not get lost amid other problems or be misdiagnosed. Some of the most unhappy treatment stories involve it being diagnosed as an eating disorder, malingering, or non-compliance with therapy.

## Anxiety Disorders

### Panic Disorder (PD): F41.0

The key characteristic of PD is that panic attacks are unexpected and without an obvious "cue or trigger" (American Psychiatric Association 2022, p. 236). Since a panic attack may happen anytime, patients can constantly become fearful without knowing when it will occur. They also tend to avoid the places and the things they were doing when a panic attack occurred.

The misdiagnosis of PD for emetophobia can come when the patient is too ashamed to admit what they are panicking about or the clinician underestimates vomiting as the central trigger. Another clue for the clinician is that the median age of onset for PD is 20–24 years (in the US) and is extremely rare before age 14 (<0.4%) (American Psychiatric Association 2022, pp. 237, 238), while emetophobia has an earlier onset, almost exclusively in childhood.

Often the beginnings of an anxiety disorder are not the same as how the disorder is maintained. For example, the original panic attacks may have been directly caused by the fear of vomiting. Over time, a fear of having a panic attack develops, and panic disorder becomes a comorbid or at least conjoined problem. It may need to be addressed as well as the emetophobia. Since a panic attack can cause stomach distress, the disorders may or may not be independent but are reinforced by one another in a distressing cycle.

### Separation Anxiety Disorder (SAD): F93.0

Often in children, but even adults, emetophobia can be confused with or co-occur with SAD. SAD is characterized by a fear that something will happen to major attachment figures or that while separated from an attachment figure, something terrible will happen to the child, such as being kidnapped, getting lost, or having an accident. Surrounding these core fears are symptoms like refusing to be apart from a parent, refusing to sleep alone, having nightmares, or experiencing severe distress anticipating separation. The difference between emetophobia and SAD is further confused by the physical complaints or symptoms associated with SAD, which may include stomach aches, nausea, and vomiting.

The core fear is relevant in determining if the primary issue is emetophobia or SAD. If the separation is almost entirely about getting sick, then emetophobia is likely the correct diagnosis. The symptoms of SAD, whether due to emetophobia or comorbid, may need to be addressed along with emetophobia during treatment.

### Agoraphobia: F40.00

A simple explanation of agoraphobia is that the patient is afraid to leave home. Sometimes it is open places, but often it is crowds that are feared, or traveling away from home for any time. It is often associated with panic disorder because the patient may have had a panic attack somewhere and is now afraid to leave the house in case it happens again.

If emetophobia is severe or complicated by the fear of embarrassing oneself by vomiting in public, the patient often will not want to leave home. It can be tricky for the clinician to diagnose emetophobia if the patient does not tell them what exactly they fear. I (Anna) once treated a patient whose world became so small with emetophobia that they would not leave their bathroom. After they refused to eat, their parents and I finally had to call authorities under the Canadian Mental Health Act to take them forcibly to a psychiatric facility.

### Social Anxiety Disorder (Social Phobia) (SP): F40.10

Many people with emetophobia are terrified of vomiting in public. Once I (Anna) was successfully treated for emetophobia, I was shocked to discover I still had a fear of vomiting in front of someone else (which many people with emetophobia describe as "in public"). I was once taken to the ER with chest pain. It turned out to be some odd epiglottal seizure, but apparently, once you're over 50, they take these things quite seriously. I was rushed in and immediately hooked up to all sorts of leads and wires. I felt nauseous, I was shaking, and a single tear rolled down my cheek. Luckily my daughter was with me. I told her, "I'm afraid to throw up in front of all these people." She quickly reminded me, "Mom. You're not scared of that anymore," and she was right. I calmed down immediately, never vomited, and the next time I felt nauseous "in public," I remained calm.

Many of our patients with emetophobia tell us they are afraid to go out to a variety of places, sometimes anywhere at all, because they might vomit. When they've told their doctors or therapists this, they were often diagnosed with social phobia. SP is indeed fear of judgment and/or embarrassing oneself in public—sometimes it's talking, walking, playing sports, blushing, using the bathroom, or even eating when other people are around. Many fear they may choke on food.

A little more probing at intake may be necessary before diagnosing a patient with SP. The clinician may need to ask the patient specifically, "what would be the worst thing that could happen to you in public?" If there's any mention of vomiting, one will want to ask a lot more about that.

In children, SP usually manifests itself in fear of being laughed at, especially by peers. A child with SP may not be anxious in front of a group of adults. In our experience, some kids previously diagnosed with SP or labeled as "shy" may be too ashamed to admit to anyone, even their parents, that they are afraid of vomiting. As a child, I (Anna) was not the least bit shy, but my emetophobia led me to severely restrict activities outside the home. I did not tell my mother until I was 26 that all the years I caused her so much stress and grief and confusion, I was afraid of vomiting. Of course, she had guessed it by that time, but having heard nothing about emetophobia in the 1960s, she assumed that my absolute terror had to be about more than just being near someone who vomited. It wasn't.

### Generalized Anxiety Disorder (GAD): F41.1

Whenever the DSM-5-TR, and therefore clinicians, use a word like "generalized," patients should be wary of them throwing it around where it doesn't belong. True GAD is difficult to diagnose, but the key, according to psychiatrist and diagnostic specialist James Morrison (2014, p. 191), is this: "The symptoms are relatively unfocused; the nervousness is low-key and chronic; panic attacks are not required."

Whitton, Luiselli, and Donaldson (2006), in treating a child with GAD and SPOV, addressed the child's anxiety and stomach aches with gradual exposure and saw significant improvement at the treatment's end. It is our opinion that the child probably only suffered from emetophobia, and the clinicians inadvertently treated her successfully by focusing on the specific phobia during treatment.

## MICHAEL

Michael was ten years old when his pediatric psychiatrist diagnosed him with GAD and prescribed medication. After six months on the medication, Michael was still asking his parents at least once *per hour* to feel his forehead to make sure he wasn't ill. He also asked his teacher to feel his forehead several times per day. Michael was nervous at school, restless, had trouble sleeping, and asked his parents questions that seemed to relate to nothing in particular: "Will I be okay on the school bus? Is grandma coming over later? Do we have to go get my sister at ballet today?" Since these questions did not seem focused, and Michael's symptoms didn't appear to relate to any other anxiety disorder (yet he was obviously anxious), the psychiatrist diagnosed GAD.

Michael had told his parents that he was afraid of sickness; he just didn't specify that it was only vomit-related sickness. However, they knew his fears began after he had been quite sick the winter before with norovirus. They stumbled upon my (Anna's) website and booked a consultation. After only a few minutes with Michael, I could discern the nature of his worry.

ANNA:      What happened on the school bus?
MICHAEL:   A kid threw up.
ANNA:      Why is it a problem if grandma comes over?
MICHAEL:   One time, she laughed so much she cried, then coughed and threw up in our sink.
ANNA:      Why don't you like getting your sister from ballet?
MICHAEL:   Her ballet friend told her she throws up in the car, and I'm worried my mom will give her a ride home if we go there.

Once Michael was diagnosed correctly with emetophobia, he did well in treatment. One of the "games" I tried with him was the "get-out-of-jail-free card," so named after the popular Monopoly™ game. I asked his parents to make five "feel my forehead for free" cards and give them to

Michael. Each time he wanted either his parents or his teacher to feel his forehead, he was to give them a card. Five cards were all he got for the week. At the following appointment, Michael had only used two of the cards the entire week. This game worked well with many of my child patients, whether it was "get out of school free," "don't ride the bus free," or "get up after bedtime for free"—the possibilities are many.

After about six sessions, Michael no longer asked his parents or teachers to feel his forehead, and I sent them on their way to work with him using Russ and McCarthy's *Turnaround: Turning Fear into Freedom* (2010) with its *Emetophobia Supplement* (2016).

Sometimes you just have to ask.


## Dissociative Disorders
### Depersonalization/Derealization Disorder: F48.1
Some people with emetophobia will describe incidents where they felt as though they were in a dream or were detached from themselves, almost as if they were dead and looking down on themselves. They are not delusional; they know that what they experienced was not reality at the time. We have found that people with emetophobia can experience depersonalization whenever the phobia is triggered, and they have a severe anxiety attack, normally with a subjective unit of distress level of 8, 9, or 10. If the core fear is about vomiting, depersonalization should be considered a result of emetophobia, or at the very least, a comorbidity.

## Somatic Symptom and Related Disorders
### Somatic Symptom Disorder (SSD): F45.1
Only one somatic symptom is necessary to meet the DSM-5-TR criteria for SSD. For emetophobia patients, this is chronic and debilitating nausea. Another criterion of SSD, as with most mental disorders, is that the condition causes distress or impairs functioning. Emetophobia fits.

Nausea in people with emetophobia is often a symptom of anxiety, as the sympathetic nervous system's response to a threat *or perceived threat* is to slow down or even shut down digestion. This leads to a feedback loop where anxiety causes nausea, which causes greater anxiety, which causes more nausea. The average person with pre-exam jitters or who dreads the thought of public speaking may experience this nausea, vomit or defecate, and feel better.

Ironically, SSD is also a condition that is often misdiagnosed. Morrison (2014, p. 252) writes:

> There is an ever-present danger that clinicians will diagnose an anxiety or mood disorder and ignore the underlying SSD. Then the all-too-common result is that the patient receives treatment specific for the mood or anxiety disorder, rather than an approach that might actually address the underlying SSD.

Clinicians' tendencies to diagnose emetophobia as SSD is often brought on by the fact that patients, particularly children, have had extensive medical diagnostic tests to uncover the reason for their chronic nausea, and their doctors have not discovered any medical cause for it. We've had it happen more than once that family doctors send a patient to us with the diagnosis of SSD already.

An accurate diagnosis of SSD would typically involve the patient being very worried about the meaning of the symptom. Adult SSD patients spend time and money on medical tests. People with emetophobia only worry that nausea will lead to vomiting and are usually afraid to go to hospitals and have medical tests. Again, ask the questions. Look for emetophobia, particularly in children, who can be more ashamed and reticent.

### Illness Anxiety Disorder (IAD): F45.21

IAD is another anxiety disorder that can be confused with emetophobia. IAD was referred to as Health Anxiety in DSM-IV and in the past, hypochondriasis, or hypochondria. Assuming the primary health concern is vomiting, we are not sure it makes a difference if this is the diagnosis other than it doesn't offer much explanation. People with emetophobia and IAD are both preoccupied with illness. With emetophobia, it is about vomiting, but in our experience with IAD, the fear is typically more about something like cancer or deadly cardiovascular events. IAD and emetophobia can cause panic, so the patient is afraid they're having a heart attack because their heart rate is so high due to the anxiety. In my (Anna's) experience, panic attacks feel like you're about to die, so it makes sense that someone would assume they had something terribly wrong with them.

In adults, a frequent way to identify IAD is multiple doctor visits. The clinician can often work with the family doctor to help the patient with IAD reduce their visits and live with the uncertainty of not knowing. A physician's reassurance works as well as any reassurance: briefly and poorly. "What if the doctor is wrong?"

Another common symptom of IAD is an almost insatiable desire to read about the feared problem online. This takes on an excessive or compulsive quality. The problem with making a differential diagnosis can be that people with emetophobia do the same thing. They go online to search for illnesses that may lead to vomiting, side effects of prescribed drugs that include vomiting, problems with foods being undercooked or left out of the fridge too long, which can lead to vomiting, and norovirus outbreaks in their area.

IAD has two subsets: care-seeking type and care-avoidant type. We also see this with emetophobia. Some patients are at the doctor's office or ER an inordinate number of times, while others avoid doctors, hospitals, and diagnostic tests to the point that their actual health can be jeopardized.

## MIN

Min came to me (Anna) after having been diagnosed with IAD by a total of seven different clinicians, which included psychiatrists (two), psychologists (two), a psychiatric nurse practitioner, a registered social worker, and a licensed counselor. The family physician who referred her to one of the psychiatrists also believed she had IAD. Min's mother and sister both had type 2 diabetes, and if their blood sugar got too low, they would vomit. Min was constantly worried that she, too, would develop diabetes and vomit when her sugar got too low. She ordered diagnostic equipment that people with diabetes use, and if her sugar level ever went below 6 mmol/L, she would become incredibly anxious and often go to the ER. (Low blood sugar is only cause for concern when sugar levels drop to 3.9 mmol/L or below.)

Luckily, Min stumbled upon my website while searching online for help with the fear of vomiting. Once we discerned that she was actually afraid of vomiting, we were able to work on doing away with the diagnostic equipment (a safety behavior), and Min began leading a more normal life. Over time, her emetophobia symptoms diminished, and she found a life partner and a new job. She had no more ER visits.

### Functional Neurologic Disorder (FND): F44.4–F44.7

Code numbers for FND depend on symptoms. Typically when we think of FND (previously called "conversion disorder"), we envision a person having seizures, hallucinations, blindness, deafness, or abnormal motor movement (stumbling, falling) *for no medical reason*. Indeed, FND cannot be diagnosed without the appropriate medical tests, which can sometimes be numerous. I (Anna) worked with one patient with emetophobia who had what I believed to be FND and severe emetophobia and OCD. They underwent numerous medical tests, which were all negative. Suggesting FND to such a patient is a delicate business. I never did, as I knew they would not only disbelieve me but also chalk me up to yet another health care provider who thought their problem was "all in their head." If there is no medical reason whatsoever for someone's FND-type symptoms and they have been diagnosed with emetophobia with or without other diagnoses, then FND is indeed a distinct possibility.

There is also another little-known symptom of FND called "swallowing symptoms." The patient sometimes describes a lump in the throat or trouble swallowing. People with emetophobia often speak of a lump in the throat as well. They usually say they feel "gaggy," and gagging terrifies them because they believe it usually precedes vomiting. The description of this lump or gaggy feeling has led some clinicians to diagnose FND when the problem is emetophobia.

### *Obsessive-Compulsive and Related Disorders (OCRD)*

### Obsessive-Compulsive Disorder (OCD): F42.2

The DSM-IV listed OCD among anxiety disorders. This made sense as patients indeed suffered a great deal of anxiety, especially if they refrained from compulsions such as washing or checking. Although it is now listed in the DSM-5 and DSM-5-TR in its own section, OCRDs, the treatment is virtually the same as that for anxiety.

The relationship between emetophobia and OCD is not well-determined because emetophobia is so under-researched. However, as with emetophobia, OCD involves serious and chronic anxiety. Everyone with emetophobia that we have treated possesses at least some characteristics of OCD. We agree with Veale, Hennig, and Gledhill (2015) that a diagnosis of comorbid OCD should only be made if there are additional obsessions or compulsions not related to vomiting. For example, there might be a fear of incontinence or checking rituals for an unrelated illness.

People with emetophobia will wash their hands until raw for fear of germs from an illness that will make them vomit. Many with emetophobia have other symptoms of OCD, such as rituals to keep from vomiting or to reassure themselves that they are not sick (i.e., compulsive temperature-taking), or superstitions about numbers and dates (especially the date they last vomited). Children may repeatedly ask for reassurance that they won't vomit. Such prediction is an impossible task for a parent, but it is usually undertaken to keep the peace.

There are numerous variations or subsets of OCD, such as contamination, checking, symmetry, fear of harming oneself or others, and fear of immoral thoughts. The most common subset is contamination, and this is the one often confused with emetophobia. Emetophobia functions very much like OCD. There is an obsession—the fear of vomiting. There are the compulsions—checking expiration dates, washing hands, monitoring one's body for signs of illness, restricting foods, or performing superstitious rituals to prevent one from vomiting.

Unlike other phobias, emetophobia can continually preoccupy the patient, like someone with OCD. The compulsions or rituals can be similarly strong. There is a notable symptom overlap with contamination OCD. In the case of emetophobia, the contaminant is almost always limited to something that would result in catching norovirus or ingesting something that would result in food poisoning.

Veale et al. (2015) conducted a preliminary study of emetophobia and OCD for "explor[ing] whether the phenomenology and co-morbidity of SPOV... might best fit within the group of obsessive compulsive and related disorders" (p. 5). They suggest that there are perhaps four different manifestations of emetophobia:

1. A milder form which is more a fear than an actual phobia and affects approximately 7 percent of women and 1.8 percent of

men (Van Hout and Bouman 2011). The criteria for a specific phobia would not be met.

2. A form that is more closely related to somatic obsessions such as the fear of losing control (of bladder or bowels), perhaps doing so in public. This form may normally have a later age of onset.

3. A form in which the patient has emetophobia and comorbid OCD, the obsessions and compulsions of which are not related to vomiting.

4. A much more severe form of comorbid OCD and emetophobia in which emetophobia is different from other phobias altogether and more akin to an OCRD. The obsessive thoughts and the contaminant-related compulsions relate to vomiting, and perhaps only to vomiting.

Keyes and Veale (2021) posit that there is a continuum between emetophobia and OCD. At one end, there is "pure" emetophobia, which is like other phobias. The other end is more like OCD in that the patient has many obsessive thoughts and repetitive behaviors. They conclude their hypothesis with, "There is no doubt there are similar processes in emetophobia and OCD, and it may be more important to focus on these rather than worry about whether it's called emetophobia or OCD" (p. 22). The continuum may look something like Figure 2.1.

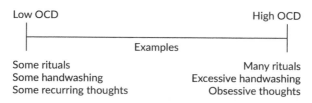

Low OCD              High OCD

Examples

Some rituals         Many rituals
Some handwashing     Excessive handwashing
Some recurring thoughts    Obsessive thoughts

**FIGURE 2.1:** OCD CONTINUUM IN EMETOPHOBIA

Many patients come to us already with a diagnosis of OCD with or without emetophobia. Sometimes this is a misdiagnosis simply because the patient washes their hands often. Other times it is evident that the patient has OCD based on specific intrusive thoughts, and rituals that may or may not be related to vomiting. We have also noted that some patients are distressed with having an OCD diagnosis added to their diagnosis of phobia, as though they have more than one thing wrong with them. A savvy clinician will reassure them that these disorders are related to one another and that the treatment is the same regardless of the diagnosis.

Some of my (David's) child patients who presented initially with emetophobia I saw again some years later, and they had symptoms of more typical OCD. The emetophobia was in remission, but the anxiety evolved to a different target fear. Usually, it is still health-related.

However, if the fear is about vomiting and the rituals/compulsions/ safety behaviors are all aimed at reducing or escaping the possibility of vomiting, then it makes more sense to consider a diagnosis of emetophobia.

## Feeding and Eating Disorders

### ANNA'S STORY—PART 5

I managed to hide emetophobia from everyone, even mom, and get through high school. I was a very selective eater, but mother made sure I ate enough to survive. Then I went away to university and lived in a dorm where of course, nobody monitored my eating. Long story short, I got to the point by the second year when all I would eat was bananas, Digestive® cookies (biscuits), and milk. This was 1976, so there was no internet and no information to be found. I looked at length for a phobia of vomiting in the psychology library, poring over stacks and stacks of books and articles. Nothing. I was convinced that I was the only person on earth who felt this way, which further solidified that I should tell no one. But one thing I did know, and that was that if I kept eating the way I was eating I was going to die.

By luck or the grace of God, I decided to design my own treatment with gradual exposure, even though I had never even heard of such a thing. I thought I would train myself to get eating again, bite by bite. I remember the first dinner was poached sole, tater tots, and broccoli with cheese sauce. I took one bite of fish, one small piece of broccoli, and one tater tot. I cried the whole time. In fact, I did a lot of crying for the next two years or so until I was eating properly again.

I will add that I told a group of my dorm friends about being afraid of food poisoning, which they seemed to understand, and so they were able to support me at meals by coaching me, reassuring me, and cheering for me when I did well. The unconditional love and support I received from them was ironically what all people with emetophobia need from the people around them, but families may be too anxious or frustrated about the emetophobia to provide it.

---

### Anorexia Nervosa (AN)—Restricting Type: F50.02[1]

One of the most common misdiagnoses of emetophobia is AN (Manassis and Kalman 1990; Veale et al. 2012). According to Veale et al. (2012, p. 417), "The correct diagnosis of SPOV is important, as patients are unlikely to identify with a treatment model for an eating disorder."

It is easy to see how emetophobia can be confused with an eating disorder because patients can be anorexic, as "anorexia" literally means "lack or loss of appetite for food." However, the word itself has become the layperson's short form of *anorexia nervosa*. People with emetophobia may be underweight, have nutritional problems, or display intense control over food. We have had more than one patient where all these issues were present. The criteria for a diagnosis of AN (restricting type), however, are three-fold (American Psychiatric Association 2022, p. 381):

1. The patient is underweight as a direct result of restricting food.
2. The patient is exceedingly concerned with weight gain.
3. The patient has a distorted view of themselves, in other words, the perception that they are overweight, even when that is clearly not the case.

People with emetophobia do not fit the second or third criteria. Some clinicians mistakenly assume that the patient is lying about that. We have had many patients, mainly adolescent girls, who were admitted to eating disorder clinics or residential programs where they were essentially force-fed and expected to endure the sound of their roommates purging. This has served only to re-traumatize the patient.

As mentioned, with emetophobia, there is often food restriction. Veale et al. (2012) found that people with emetophobia who restricted their food intake had higher scores on the SPOVI and were more likely to experience nausea frequently. It might be that only certain "safe"

---

1   F50.01 Binge-eating/purging type is seldom a misdiagnosis of emetophobia for obvious reasons.

foods are eaten. It is important to determine why this is the case. Someone could merely be a selective (or the more pejorative term, "picky") eater. This is especially true of children.

People with emetophobia also often limit the amount of food they eat. They tell us that if they're going to vomit, they want to minimize the amount of food that would be vomited, or they believe small amounts of food will minimize nausea. For the same reason, they will also stop eating before they feel full. Sometimes patients will eat small bites with long periods of time in between. Often this is done in secret because it is so incongruous with how other people eat. The point of that may be to test each bite to see if it causes a problem or not.

I (David) have had a least one case where AN was comorbid with emetophobia. I have rarely encountered such a catch-22. While she really wanted to be less fearful of eating, as she succeeded, she would gain unwanted weight. She found the fear (not at its worst) beneficial in keeping weight down. Improvement of one condition made the other worse. *When a patient, particularly a child, stops eating altogether or loses significant weight it is a medical emergency.*

### Avoidant/Restrictive Food Intake Disorder (ARFID): F50.89

From the heading, it is clear to see why ARFID is often confused with emetophobia. The common characteristics of ARFID are an apparent lack of interest in eating, avoiding food because of unpleasant sensory aspects, or a concern about some sort of negative consequence of eating. Most often seen in children, ARFID patients are underweight and sometimes need hospitalization.

Some people with emetophobia do lose interest in food and are certainly worried about possible negative consequences of eating. They can have significant and even dangerous weight loss. What is missing from an ARFID diagnosis is the fear of vomiting. With emetophobia, the characteristics of ARFID result from the underlying fear rather than a lack of interest in food. It is possible that there may be sensory issues as well, but if the fear of vomiting were not present then you would simply have a selective eater. Someone with emetophobia may absolutely meet the criteria for ARFID, but the diagnosis would be incorrect because *the symptoms are better explained by another mental disorder*.

Our patients who were mistakenly taken to residential or partial hospitalization programs for eating disorders felt the educational content and cognitive interventions were not relevant to them and that they were treated as being resistant or in denial if they disagreed.

## Mood Disorders
### Bipolar II Disorder: F31.81 [296.89]
It is doubtful that any clinician would diagnose a person with emetophobia with bipolar I disorder, as an essential criterion is at least one manic episode, something which people with emetophobia rarely if ever describe. However, we do come across patients who have been diagnosed with bipolar II. Since depression is often comorbid with anxiety disorders and emetophobia is no exception, this box can easily get ticked.

The only other criterion for bipolar II is "hypomania" (mild mania). People with emetophobia feel good when they're not nauseous, or they're not doing anything that would trigger their fear. If they have a naturally upbeat personality these times might resemble hypomania when, in fact, they are more akin to relief. When they do feel sick, especially if they suffer comorbid depression, their mood can quickly go downhill. We are still aghast at how many clinicians refuse to take their patients' word for it and come up with far-reaching diagnoses simply because they've never heard of emetophobia and can't believe that anyone's symptoms could be so severe "just from being afraid to vomit."

### Disruptive Mood Dysregulation Disorder (DMDD): F34.8
DMDD can only be diagnosed in children ages 6–17. The symptoms are frequent with severe tantrums (three or more per week), persistent negative mood (angry, sad, miserable), and lasting for at least one year. AMDD is akin to the disorders described next with the difference being that the child has a depressed or negative mood between episodes.

## Disruptive, Impulse-Control and Conduct Disorders
### Oppositional Defiant Disorder (ODD): F91.3
Far too many children with emetophobia that I (Anna) have worked with have been misdiagnosed with ODD. I'm quite sure that if there had been such a diagnosis in 1968, they would have stamped it on my forehead as well. I was probably the worst kind because I refused to tell anyone that I was afraid of being where someone might vomit.

Once, when it came time to board a school bus, I saw the teacher handing out bags to all the kids who got motion sick. Let's just say I was oppositional and defiant. Nothing short of Dwayne Johnson and three of his friends could have gotten me onto that bus with all the screaming, punching, and kicking I was doing.

ODD is characterized by arguing with parents or authority figures, often angrily, as well as refusal to obey rules. Kids with ODD may have angry outbursts where they can fly off the handle and destroy things if they are challenged. They must have symptoms for more than six months and the symptoms must disrupt their education/work or social and personal lives. Let us illustrate how emetophobia was misdiagnosed as ODD in the story of Bobby.

## BOBBY

I (Anna) met this delightful ten-year-old child after he had been expelled from school for fits of screaming and turning over tables and chairs in his classroom. His parents had known he was afraid of vomiting for the past four years. They describe it as beginning after a nasty bout of norovirus at around that time. After the Jesus-in-the-temple incident, Bobby was taken to a psychiatrist who diagnosed him with ODD and GAD.

Bobby had become so anxious about vomiting by seven years old that he refused to go to school. He had panic attacks when separating from his mom or dad. In third grade, he would only attend school if his mother sat at the back of the classroom, and eventually if she promised to sit in her car in the school parking lot until classes were dismissed. Bobby made numerous trips to the school nurse complaining of stomach aches. In fourth grade his parents and teachers decided they should just make him deal with it, so mom dropped him at the door and the principal half-dragged Bobby to his classroom, screaming and crying. After only a short time in class, Bobby complained to the teacher that he had a stomach ache and wanted to go see the nurse. The teacher refused to let him leave the classroom, which is what led Bobby to begin turning over desks and chairs. I saw him with his parents just a few days later.

After meeting this child on intake, suffice it to say that if his parents didn't want him anymore, I would have taken him home. He was adorable, smart, funny, and well-mannered. Of course, his parents did want him—they were as lovely as he was. After hearing the story, I turned to Bobby, showing my delight at having a conversation with him. My demeanor was almost joking with him:

ANNA:      Sounds like you were pretty upset.
BOBBY:    (sheepishly) Ya.
ANNA:      You must have been really scared, huh?
BOBBY:    Ya. I don't know what I was thinking.
ANNA:      *Were you* thinking?
BOBBY:    I... guess not?

I smiled and chuckled a bit.

ANNA:      What was so scary?
BOBBY:    Just my mom not being there and not feeling good, and I wanted to leave.
ANNA:      Have you ever heard of "fight or flight?"
BOBBY:    No.
ANNA:      Well, when people *or animals* get really really scared, they do two things: they fight, or they take flight, which means they run for their lives. So, if a rabbit sees a wolf, it will hop as fast as it can to get away, but if the wolf catches the rabbit, it will fight that wolf by biting and kicking until it's dead. Same with people. If a bear starts running towards us in the woods, we'll run like mad. You can't outrun a bear so eventually it will catch you, and when it does you will fight and fight and fight until you're dead. Or the bear runs off. So, it sounds to me like what was happening to you is that you were *so scared* that you wanted to run, like out of the classroom or home, but they didn't let you run, so you got angry and started breaking up the furniture and *then* they let you go home. Sound about right?
BOBBY:    (*with a big grin*) Ya. They sure let me go home after I did that!

We all laughed.

ANNA:      Okay, so this tells me two things: (turning to his parents) one, his emetophobia is pretty severe, and two, he doesn't have ODD.

The collective exhale in the room was palpable.

ANNA: Okay, Bobby, so we're going to figure out some better ways to cope with your fear, and I'll talk to your teachers, and then I'm pretty sure they'll let you back into school.

Bobby did well in treatment, as we find most children do. After ten sessions with me, he returned to school and separated from his mother without incident. He made no trips to the school nurse for the remainder of the year, and his teacher described him on his final report card as "a pleasure to have in class."

### Intermittent Explosive Disorder (IED): F63.81

If one is going to misdiagnose emetophobia as an impulse-control disorder, IED would probably be more fitting than ODD *if one were to look only at behavior*, and not the cause. With IED there is no rational cause for a person to hurl a jar of peanut butter at the cat. When a person with emetophobia like Bobby flew into a rage, however, there was an obvious reason even if his behavior did not appear to fit the situation. Outbursts of rage with IED "are unplanned, have no goal, and are excessive for the provocation" (Morrison 2014, p. 385).

## *Personality Disorders*
### Borderline Personality Disorder (BPD): F60.3

A diagnosis of BPD can be incredibly harmful to a person with emetophobia, and unfortunately, it happens. Although there should be no judgment of anyone with any type of mental illness, for some reason those with personality disorders are often judged harshly.

Much like those with severe cases of emetophobia, people with BPD are often in a state of unceasing crisis. They tend to worship you or hate you, often swinging from one to the other. If they hate you, they can manifest intense anger toward you that is both uncontrolled and inappropriate. They might engage in non-suicidal self-injury (NSSI) such as cutting, pinching, or scratching themselves. Their goal is probably to show others how desperate they are, and not to "just get attention."

Young people with emetophobia may be so terrified they will vomit that when they experience nausea, they behave shockingly. Clinicians and caregivers commonly have a hard time believing that anyone would behave that way "just because they're afraid of vomiting." "Tabitha" was one such patient of Anna.

## TABITHA

When I first met Tabitha, I was struck by what a beautiful young woman she was in every way. She was kind, intelligent, and funny, with the sort of personality you'd want in a best friend. In many ways she was very mature. Our first session took place when she was still in the psychiatric unit of a hospital.

Tabitha had been shuffled around from one type of care to another. Along the way, she had collected an assortment of diagnoses. Emetophobia was among them, but it was not seen as primary. Tabitha was diagnosed with panic disorder, generalized anxiety disorder, histrionic disorder, malingering, and finally, after an angry outburst with caregivers, BPD. She was forced into a program of dialectical behavior therapy (DBT) for 12 weeks. DBT is an excellent treatment protocol for those with BPD, suicidal individuals, and people with addictions. Its efficacy has not been established for emetophobia. Tabitha was accused of not taking it seriously since she didn't get better. In fact, she got so much worse that she took drastic measures during panic attacks such as NSSIs and feigned suicide attempts to convince the people around her she needed help.

A slew of psychiatrists diagnosed Tabitha with various mental illnesses and prescribed all manner of drugs: SSRIs, antipsychotics, mood stabilizers, anti-emetics, painkillers, and a benzodiazepine (Valium). She was taking all these drugs together when I met her. The Valium was about the only thing that helped. She was prescribed two per day. During one particularly severe panic attack, a mental health team came to her home when Tabitha called 911. They told her to take a third Valium that evening, which she did, and it helped her to calm down.

After the mental health team's report from that night, the folks in charge of her overall care finally heard her when she said she had emetophobia and that it was the underlying cause of all her behavior. They told her she could receive ten sessions of CBT from a psychotherapist intern (who had no experience treating emetophobia), but only—get this—if she agreed to stop taking the Valium altogether. Tabitha said that the Valium was the only thing keeping her anxiety from being completely out of control and she didn't think she could just give it up. They then sent her to a compulsory Narcotics Anonymous program. *This is how bad misdiagnosing emetophobia can get.*

Unfortunately, Tabitha's mental health problems were too numbered and complicated for me to be able to help her with my short CBT educational program. She did agree to see a local psychiatrist familiar with emetophobia. She stated that Tabitha may have some symptoms of BPD when it comes to emotion regulation, but that severe emetophobia was her primary diagnosis.

## Miscellaneous Issues
### Malingering: Z76.5

This must be one of the most insulting, defeating, hopelessness-inducing diagnoses a clinician can give to a patient with emetophobia. The diagnosis has taken many forms, both in my own (Anna's) personal experience and in our experience with patients who miraculously try therapy again. Here's a short list of some common things that clinicians have said to me and to other people with emetophobia, by their report:

- You're making this up to get attention or to avoid something else you should be doing.
- You're just non-compliant.
- You obviously don't want to get better.
- Where did you get that word, "emetophobia?" Is it even a word?
- Nobody likes to vomit. You're just being silly.
- It's all in your head.
- This isn't a real disorder. You just need to vomit once, and you'll be fine. (*They won't be fine.*)
- Why are you carrying around peppermint oil and sniffing it? Do you know how ridiculous you look?
- I think we should just give you some ipecac syrup and induce

vomiting. Then you'll know it's nothing to be afraid of. (*What do they suggest to patients who fear getting cancer?*)

Most clinicians are still unaware of emetophobia or fail to understand its particular nature and severity. Misdiagnosis, unfortunately, can lead to incorrect treatment, victim-blaming, and a patient's lack of confidence in the psychotherapeutic and medical community. When clinicians first engage with a patient who fears vomiting, we must be very cautious about our diagnosis. We should also be asking ourselves if former diagnoses by other clinicians of this patient are correct. While emetophobia is relatively easy to diagnose, it is often overlooked as the cause of such severe symptoms of avoidance or safety behaviors.

*— Chapter 3 —*

# MEDICAL CONDITIONS AND COMORBIDITIES

## Medical Conditions

Many people with emetophobia have been diagnosed with physical ailments, normally those that affect the gastrointestinal (GI) system. This phenomenon is so prevalent among our combined patients with emetophobia that it is worth taking the time to make note of it. Some patients diagnose themselves with these various disorders, but most have been diagnosed by their physicians. We, of course, are not physicians and our comments should be viewed with that in mind.

If there is an underlying medical reason for nausea, esophageal, or other digestive distress or pain, then of course it must be treated accordingly by the medical community. In this case, emetophobia treatment alone can remove the excess fear but not the physical symptoms.

If there is a medical condition and if it is treated successfully then it can make the emetophobia treatment process much easier and faster. The connection between the gut and the brain seems to be becoming clearer and new findings appear regularly. However, determining what is anxiety and what is digestive functioning is complicated. Although we recommend a thorough physical exam, many patients are too afraid to have them in case one of the tests causes vomiting. This lack of a medical evaluation can interfere with successful psychological treatment as there may be a comorbid medical condition that needs addressing as well.

### Gastroesophageal Reflux Disease (GERD)

GERD can present in infants all the way to older adults. It is the result of a weak or malfunctioning esophageal sphincter so that acid from the stomach comes up the esophagus (Kia and Hirano 2015). The symptoms are often a burning feeling (heartburn), acid literally coming up in a burp, trouble swallowing, sore throat, cough, or even chest pain. (Chest pain should always be treated as a medical emergency, especially at first, regardless of one's thought that it's just indigestion.)

The treatment for GERD is normally medication—everything from mild antacids to prescribed proton pump inhibitors. A change in diet is often recommended as well: to smaller meals and limiting alcohol, caffeine, and any foods that seem obvious to you that cause an episode. Imagine if you added to this simple problem anxiety so terrifying that you felt as if you were going to die at any moment. A case of GERD can send a person with emetophobia running to the doctor for a diagnosis and any treatment at all that would stop the episode from ever happening again.

### Eosinophilic Esophagitis (EoE)

The first diagnostic guidelines for EoE were published in 2007 (Spergel et al. 2018). Although considered rare, it affects both children and adults and is increasing in prevalence, affecting one out of 2000 people and occurring slightly more often in males. Common symptoms include abdominal pain, food impaction, difficulty swallowing, vomiting, chest pain, and failure to thrive (APFED 2022; Odze 2009). According to APFED, EoE is a chronic allergic inflammatory disease. For reasons still unknown, but possibly due to a food allergy, white blood cells build up in the esophagus. It is diagnosed by endoscopy and if white blood cells are not visible at first, then a biopsy is done to look for them. Even with a biopsy, white blood cells may not be present in EoE, which is where it gets tricky for people with emetophobia. The treatment is a change in diet to eliminate the most common allergens, as well as medication.

### MATT

When I (David) think of Matt, I think of his determination. I met him when he was 12. He was neurologically divergent and had challenges with fine motor skills. He has a condition called prosopagnosia, wherein people cannot recognize faces. To top it all off, for the previous three years Matt had been reeling from emetophobia. Most kids with emetophobia are very attached to an adult who makes them feel safer. When the phobia was bad, he was terrified of being in public and not being able to recognize a "safe face" or finding the safe adult. He and a parent drove close to two hours for every session, one way.

Because of his determination, Matt made steady headway with the emetophobia. He became less symptomatic and really worked hard on the homework. However, there was one symptom that stubbornly persisted. He would get very anxious about choking or food getting stuck in his throat. His overall fear of vomiting was much better, but not this. When every other aspect of the anxiety gets better except for one feature, it is worth further examination. Like many kids with emetophobia, he had a GI doctor. The doctor suspected there was something physical going on apart from the phobia. Matt had an endoscopy with biopsies and was diagnosed with EoE, which includes difficulty swallowing. People with EoE are also more susceptible to infection and so we had a whole discussion about what are legitimate precautions and what are safety behaviors. Sometimes anxiety signals legitimate problems that require decisions and planning. Sometimes the signal is excessive and the resulting safety behaviors are unnecessary and targets for treatment. Once he was treated for emetophobia, understood EoE, and made the necessary dietary changes, Matt's fear, and the sensation itself, significantly dropped.

## Gastric Ulcers

It was a long-held belief, particularly by laypeople, that ulcers were caused by stress or by a combination of stress and spicy or difficult-to-digest food. We now know that ulcers, which are sores in the stomach lining, are almost always caused by the presence of *H. pylori* bacteria (Sung et al. 1995). Despite this knowledge being fairly prevalent, some people with emetophobia believe that their anxiety is causing ulcers.

The symptoms of gastric ulcers are nausea, loss of appetite, and pain in the stomach or even the small intestine. These symptoms are indicative of many other gastric diseases *and also of anxiety*. Ulcers, like many other diseases of the GI tract, are diagnosed by endoscopy or a barium swallow test. Both tests can be terrifying to a person with emetophobia, as they often believe that barium will make them vomit, and either the endoscopy tube or the sedation used for an endoscopy will make them gag or vomit. Many emetophobic patients' ulcers go untreated, even though the treatment is normally as simple as a round of antibiotics. Some patients have managed to convince their physicians to try the antibiotics without the tests, but that is not very common, and for good reason.

### Gastroparesis

According to Enweluzo and Aziz (2013), gastroparesis is a condition where the muscles of the digestive tract are slow or stop altogether so the stomach does not empty properly. The result is a feeling of fullness (even when the stomach is not at all full), acid reflux, pain, and nausea. The cause of gastroparesis is not wholly known but viral infections, damage to the vagus nerve in surgery or by accident, some medications, and some autoimmune disorders such as scleroderma may lead to it.

The result of chronic gastroparesis is nutritional deficiency, poor appetite, weight loss, and problems controlling blood sugar. Many women who present to their doctors with symptoms of gastroparesis as well as anxiety are often diagnosed with only anxiety (anxiety can also cause slow motility) and sent away—a well-documented phenomenon that disproportionately happens with women, and even more so with women of color.

Diagnostic tests for gastroparesis include upper GI series, endoscopy, barium swallow, ultrasound, and a gastric emptying test (Stein, Everhart, and Lacy 2015). Each one of these tests presents problems for the person with emetophobia. If they are fortunate enough to be seeing a therapist before these tests are recommended, the therapist can write a letter to the medical providers describing their fears and recommending sedation and anti-emetics. Gastroparesis may be treated with changes in diet, medication, and/or surgery in the most extreme of cases. At times a jejunostomy tube must be inserted for bypassing the stomach and feeding the patient who may have become seriously underweight. Metoclopramide (Reglan) speeds up motility but can have serious side effects. Erythromycin is often prescribed but it can lose its effectiveness over time (Bouras et al. 2013).

Sometimes medication is prescribed only to relieve symptoms of nausea and vomiting: prochlorperazine (Compro), diphenhydramine (Benedryl), or ondansetron (Zofran). People with emetophobia are usually thrilled to get one of the latter prescriptions. Unfortunately, they may not even have gastroparesis: it can be that anxiety is slowing down their motility, in which case the medication serves only as a safety behavior. On the flip side of this, some patients with emetophobia have gastroparesis (confirmed with diagnostics) but for some reason don't vomit, and they have been told by clinicians that if they are not vomiting, then it can't be gastroparesis.

### Inflammatory Bowel Disease (IBD)

According to the Crohn's and Colitis Federation of America (2020), IBD takes two forms: Crohn's and ulcerative colitis. The latter affects the large intestine, while Crohn's can affect any part of the GI tract. IBD is not to be confused with IBS (irritable bowel syndrome) as IBD is usually much more serious. The symptoms of IBD are mainly pain and diarrhea, but patients can also experience fever, bleeding, fatigue, and weight loss. Sometimes there are even complications of the eyes, joints, skin, bones, kidneys, or liver with these diseases. Both are immune disorders, much like EoE.

As with other stomach and bowel disorders, IBD is diagnosed by endoscopy, colonoscopy, or CT/MRI with contrast. Treatment for IBD normally involves medication: aminosalicylates, corticosteroids, antibiotics, or immunomodulators. If the inflammation and damage to the GI tract is extensive enough surgery may be indicated.

### Median Arcuate Ligament Syndrome (MALS)

According to Huynh et al. (2019), MALS is a disease caused by the median arcuate ligament sitting lower than usual and therefore pressing on the celiac artery. This slows blood flow to the digestive system and also presses on nerves. The result is a great deal of pain. MALS can be asymptomatic for a time. It mostly affects thin, young women. As with other GI diseases, MALS can cause nausea, diarrhea, and pain which is worse after eating.

MALS is difficult to diagnose since the symptoms can mimic gallstones, other digestive problems, or liver disease. Gastroenterologists must rule out IBD, GERD, gallstones, gastritis, etc. To do this, a number of diagnostic tests are indicated such as X-rays, ultrasound, endoscopy, CT, or MRA (magnetic resonance angiogram) all of which may frighten a person with emetophobia. If MALS is diagnosed, surgery is usually indicated.

### Superior Mesenteric Artery Syndrome (SMAS)

According to Lippl et al. (2002), SMAS can also be called Wilkie's syndrome, mesenteric root syndrome, and a couple of other names. It is a complicated condition wherein the duodenum is compressed by the superior mesenteric artery and the abdominal aorta. It often occurs in children, mainly girls and young women aged 10–30. Since these girls and women are notoriously slim, sometimes even emaciated, it is often misdiagnosed as an eating disorder.

The symptoms of SMAS are nausea, vomiting, abdominal pain, acid reflux, and abdominal distention. Severe malnutrition can occur, which makes the problem much worse as the thinner the patient is, the worse the compression. Many SMAS patients fear eating which again makes them suspect for an eating disorder. There is some genetic predisposition to SMAS which may aid in diagnosis. A person with emetophobia with a diagnosis of this disease will be in great distress, and by the time they get to psychotherapy they may have already been discounted and/or misdiagnosed a number of times by the medical community.

The treatment for SMAS in pediatric patients is a nasogastric tube to ease the compression and potentially a jejunal feeding tube for nutrition and weight gain. Young adults may also be prescribed a feeding tube, and if the malnutrition is severe enough, total parenteral nutrition (TPN) may need to be administered via an IV or PICC line. Surgery may also be indicated in some cases.

### Irritable Bowel Syndrome (IBS)

According to the Mayo Clinic (2022):

> Irritable bowel syndrome (IBS) is a common disorder that affects the large intestine. Signs and symptoms include cramping, abdominal pain, bloating, gas, and diarrhea or constipation, or both. IBS is a chronic condition that you'll need to manage long term. Only a small number of people with IBS have severe signs and symptoms. Some people can control their symptoms by managing diet, lifestyle, and

stress. More severe symptoms can be treated with medication and counseling.

The diagnosis of IBS may at times be a catch-all for digestive problems that are not otherwise explained. The Mayo Clinic carefully suggests that "stress" can be a factor in IBS, and that "counseling" can be part of a comprehensive treatment plan. Counseling, biofeedback, relaxation, and mindfulness are listed as the only four aspects of the prevention of IBS. Lydiard et al. (1986) explored whether panic disorder could present as IBS which probably means that many health practitioners were asking the same question. While we don't doubt that IBS is a real disorder unrelated to anxiety, we nevertheless are cognizant of the fact that IBS can also be caused by and/or related to anxiety. Many of our patients (although certainly not all), upon being successfully treated for their emetophobia, have expressed to us that their IBS went away as well.

## Leaky Gut Syndrome

Leaky gut syndrome is not recognized by the medical/scientific community as a bona fide condition. The alternative health community diagnoses it and recommends vitamin supplements, herbal remedies, and special diets, often at great expense to the patient. Allegedly, the bowel wall "leaks" toxins that infiltrate the bloodstream making the patient sick. Alternative medicine clinicians and researchers claim that leaky gut syndrome causes everything from chronic fatigue syndrome to autism. At the time of writing, we are unaware of scientific evidence for these claims.

## Food Allergies, Sensitivities, and Special Diets

Many people with emetophobia are on special diets. We notice that children have had special diets suggested to them by their pediatricians who are puzzled over what is making the child feel nauseous all the time. Adult patients often diagnose themselves with celiac disease, food allergies, or the "inability to digest _____." As a result, people with emetophobia are often gluten-free, dairy-free, high-fiber, low-fiber, lactose-intolerant, FODMAP, Keto, vegetarian, or vegan. They tell us they cannot digest meat or gluten or dairy or raw vegetables or fiber. We've seen and heard it all. Some of them are accurate; others are just plain scared.

As with every other human being on the planet, people with emetophobia have "noisy bodies." Most of us just go with the flow: we ignore it and carry on. People with emetophobia cannot or will not. They fear every feeling out of the ordinary. A lot of them rush to the internet to describe their "symptoms" and ask for reassurance from their friends or on social media. Many ask their parents or significant others, sometimes as much as on an hourly basis.

### Idiopathic Nausea and Digestive Problems

When the cause of the nausea/digestive problems is unknown, the treatment, at best, is addressing the symptoms. We have seen many patients whose physicians have prescribed anti-emetic medication as strong as ondansetron without knowing the cause of the patient's nausea. Often the prescribed medication works, but we still do not know whether it works by simply calming the patient's anxiety about potentially vomiting (placebo effect).

Some physicians refuse to prescribe anti-emetic medication when they don't know the cause of the nausea. As a result, many people with emetophobia turn to over-the-counter medications such as Dramamine (Gravol), Pepto Bismol, or Tums. Some carry a "safety kit" in their purse or backpack containing these medications "just in case," while others take them habitually.

### Retrograde Cricopharyngeal Dysfunction (R-CPD)

R-CPD is the inability to burp due to a type of deformity in the upper esophageal sphincter, which cannot relax to release the air bubbles. We are unaware of any scientific evidence or studies done on R-CPD and emetophobia, but from anecdotal evidence it seems as if many people with emetophobia have this disorder. People with emetophobia also remark that they are in online groups for R-CPD and that there are several members there with emetophobia. The connection could be that trapped gas leads to discomfort and nausea.

One treatment is Botox injected into the sphincter muscle which weakens it for a few months. This may eliminate the problem or at least make it much better. After this treatment, one can burp and keep practicing burping so that when the Botox wears off, one can still do it. Some people with less severe R-CPD can learn to burp without the Botox and, after a lot of practice, they can do it well enough to eliminate the problem. Those suffering from emetophobia as well as R-CPD may feel much relief once they receive treatment. Burping will help diminish their feelings of nausea and bloating which can be very triggering of anxiety.

### Cricopharyngeus Spasm

A frequent symptom that people with emetophobia describe is an uncomfortable sensation in the throat. There is a muscle (sphincter) that surrounds the top of the esophagus that is always in a contracted state. Normally, it is not the focus of one's attention. It only relaxes when a person swallows. Sometimes, the muscle will spasm and it feels uncomfortable. The sensation is felt in the middle or lower part of the neck. People describe it as choking, pressure, tightness, or as feeling swollen. The feeling improves when someone swallows, causing the muscles to relax. Often people with emetophobia interpret this as a signal of impending vomit. Treatment might include correct diagnosis, physical therapy, a muscle relaxant, or an injection of Botox (Bastian 2022).

### Pediatric Autoimmune Neuropsychiatric Disorders Associated with Streptococcal Infection (PANDAS)

PANDAS is a peculiar disorder with which every clinician should be familiar, although it is rare and often misdiagnosed. The understanding, diagnosis, and treatment of PANDAS is rapidly changing. If left untreated, it can severely affect a neurotypical child and lead to the disruption of family life.

First identified by Swedo et al. (1998), PANDAS is a sudden and dramatic onset of symptoms that are exactly like OCD or tic disorders normally associated with Tourette syndrome. Accompanying symptoms may be separation or other anxiety, irritability, major depression as well as a host of others previously atypical for the child. The sudden onset of symptoms always follows an infection of group A streptococcus (GAS). *This infection can be asymptomatic*, which further complicates the likelihood of a correct diagnosis. "Sudden onset" often means that parents can identify the exact day when the child's behavior changed.

The pathology of PANDAS is fascinating. As described by Swedo et al. (2015), GAS triggers an autoimmune response that targets neurons in the brain, literally changing the child's behavior overnight. PANDAS affects kids from three years of age to about 12, 75 percent of whom are boys. Following puberty, children appear not to be affected by it. Kids who previously had OCD can experience a worsening of symptoms just as suddenly.

Diagnosis of PANDAS involves a throat or perianal swab for a current infection, or a blood test for antibodies that would confirm a recent streptococcal infection. Unfortunately, many parents who are aware of PANDAS may need to fight with medical providers for these tests as PANDAS is considered rare, and many clinicians are unfamiliar with it. In America, diagnosis and treatment of PANDAS can be costly as it may involve a pediatrician, rheumatologist, neurologist, infectious disease specialist, psychotherapist, psychiatrist, immunologist, or a PANDAS specialist. Insurance companies in the United States are often reluctant to recognize that all these people are necessary. Most children with PANDAS can recover with early antibiotic treatment, while some may need long-term treatment. Left untreated, PANDAS increases the risk of having tic disorders or OCD into adulthood.

Despite PANDAS being a rare condition, we both have experience with more than one patient diagnosed with it. As emetophobia is so under-researched, we do not yet know exactly how PANDAS affects previously diagnosed children, or whether PANDAS itself can lead to sudden onset of emetophobia or worsen the symptoms. The Pandas Physicians Network diagnostic guidelines (2022) list restricted food intake as part of one of the four essential symptom clusters required to make the diagnosis. Specifically, they note that fears of choking or vomiting may drive the food restriction. Part of every clinician's history-taking should be asking whether the child or their siblings have had a group A staphylococcus infection in the recent past. More research is clearly needed on PANDAS and emetophobia.

## Comorbidities

The term "comorbidity" was coined in 1970 by A.R. Feinstein as the study of the inter-relationship of different illnesses that occur simultaneously in the same person. Here we discuss three of the most common diagnoses comorbid with emetophobia. However, it is possible that patients may have any number of comorbid psychological or medical conditions.

## Depression

The unique relationship between anxiety disorders and major depressive disorder (MDD) has been studied for many years, and hotly debated. Brown and Barlow, in a large sample study (N=468) found that "50% of patients with a principal anxiety disorder had at least one clinically significant anxiety or depressive disorder" (1992, p. 838). Levey et al. (2020), in a large study of over 200,000 in the "million veteran program," found genetic links for anxiety as well as high comorbidity between anxiety, PTSD, and depression.

Anxiety disorders are the most frequent of all psychiatric disorders, with an incidence rate of about 31 percent of all Americans reporting being diagnosed with one in their lifetime (National Institute of Mental Health 2022). However, most clinicians describe treating anxiety as a comorbid disorder more often than just MDD alone. Anxiety and depression are like two sides of a pancake, meaning that they are very closely related. People may be diagnosed with just one or sometimes both. Current thought is still, nevertheless, to treat each as a separate disorder (Spijker, Muntingh, and Batelaan 2020). Emetophobia almost always has an early onset, whereas depression is more likely to appear later.

If the clinician suspects depression, a careful and thorough assessment must be done, perhaps using a standard inventory such as the Beck Depression Inventory. Many people with emetophobia, in our experience, say things such as "I don't want to/can't live like this," or "I would rather die than vomit." Despite little evidence that people with emetophobia are at risk for suicide, it's still important for the clinician to do a risk assessment. If the clinician discerns that the patient is in immediate danger, they should follow protocols in their country/state/province for reporting of risk to harm oneself. If the risk is assessed as mild, then the clinician might discuss anti-depressant medication with the patient and refer them back to their primary physician or a psychiatrist.

Here are the three most important questions to ask:

1. Sounds like you may be thinking of ending it all. Is that true?
2. Have you ever thought about *how* you would do it?
3. Have you made any *plans*?

I (Anna) have never had any person with emetophobia answer affirmatively to any of the above, except for Larry.

## LARRY

Larry was a 35-year-old highly intelligent patient with emetophobia who was also under an incredible amount of stress at work. With a deadline-driven job, Larry often stayed up until 4 am trying to finish various work projects. One day he came right out with the answer to Question 1. "Sometimes I think I should just end it all."

"Oh wow," I said. "Have you thought about how you'd do it?"

"I guess the only sure way is to use a gun." Before I had time to ask the third question, he continued. "But then I'd have to go get a gun. I don't even know where. And then fill out forms and register it and everything. I don't have time for all that!" he moaned.

Once Larry got on a couple of prescribed anti-depressants his mood was much lighter and his outlook more hopeful. When I reminded him of the previous conversation a few months later he laughed heartily.

Treatment for comorbid emetophobia and depression can be tricky to navigate. On the one hand, obviously, if the patient is in immediate danger of suicide, then the depression must be addressed. Also, depressed patients are by nature less enthusiastic about treatment and often feel hopeless about the outcomes. Lack of motivation is a *symptom* of depression, so patients are often unable to complete homework assignments and treatment will stagnate. Nevertheless, many clinicians treat depression and ignore emetophobia, probably because they are more familiar with depression and its treatment. The current school of thought is that treatment should be directed first toward the more clinically significant disorder (Spijker, Muntingh, and Batelaan 2020).

## OCD

Every one of our patients has presented with symptoms characteristic of OCD which, as we discussed in Chapter 2, is somehow connected to emetophobia. The current gold standard in OCD diagnosis is the Yale-Brown OCD Scale (Y-BOCS) which will give the clinician a good idea of how severe the OCD is. Both adult and child instruments are readily available online.

Treatment for comorbid OCD and emetophobia must focus on both disorders at the same time. Exposure and response prevention, as outlined in Chapter 6, is the treatment of choice. Along with making a hierarchy or list of emetophobic feared activities, the clinician will also include in the hierarchy all the OCD compulsions and safety behaviors so that they can be systematically eliminated. Sometimes it is necessary to treat OCD with pharmaceuticals, if the patient will tolerate them, so a referral to a primary care physician or psychiatrist will be necessary for moderate to severe OCD patients.

### Post-Traumatic Stress Disorder (PTSD): F43.10

PTSD is characterized by repeatedly reliving a traumatizing event, either in dreams, almost hallucinogenic flashbacks, depersonalization or derealization, or intrusive thoughts. The patient may go to great lengths to avoid anything which may trigger a memory of the event. Many become depressed, while still others are excessively anxious or irritable. Most people think of PTSD as being associated with war veterans, and indeed the disorder is disturbingly prevalent among them. However, survivors of many other kinds of trauma also experience PTSD.

Some emetophobia patients relate a traumatic past with stories such as those of physical or sexual abuse, confinement, torture, or various forms of experiencing the death of loved ones. Clinicians may not understand the significance of the comorbid diagnosis of emetophobia and will seek to treat the PTSD while ignoring the emetophobia. This will probably prove impossible. Nevertheless, treatment for the two disorders may happen at the same time, as exposure and response prevention is indicated for both. Normally, in our experience at least, working on exposure for emetophobia will trigger the PTSD symptoms. Patients may be unwilling to even speak of their memories of vomiting because recalling these memories triggers an incredible amount of anxiety. Nevertheless, a slow and steady approach by a compassionate clinician will eventually result in progress toward recovering from both disorders.

## Chapter 4

# ANXIETY DISORDERS AND THEIR TREATMENT

## History

Anxiety disorders are the most frequent of all psychiatric disorders with an incidence rate of about 31 percent (National Institute of Mental Health 2022). Perhaps anxiety's incidence and prevalence are so large because, from an evolutionary perspective, our ancestors were the ones who hid in caves while the brave ones who battled tigers, or one another, were killed. Whatever the reason, it may just take another five million years of evolution before our brains figure out that a true threat and a perceived threat are two different things.

As far back as the Stone Age, people have been seeking to help or treat others suffering from various forms of mental illness, including anxiety. The early shamans chipped or bore holes in the skulls of individuals suffering headaches, seizures, or what we now know are panic attacks. Anxious people, as well as those with psychoses, were often thought to be possessed by demons, and needed exorcisms. If that didn't work, they were usually thrown into crude prison cells or even executed. Some thought they might be possessed by good or magical spirits and were treated with awe and respect.

In ancient Greece, Hippocrates, considered the father of modern medicine, came to believe that mental illness was indeed pathological. He classified mental disorders such as phrenitis, mania, and melancholia. Hippocrates suggested those with melancholia lead a tranquil life without alcohol and on a vegetarian diet. He recounts the story of Nicanor. When Nicanor heard a flute, "masses of terrors rose up" (Crocq 2015). He was clearly describing a phobic reaction.

The Latin philosopher Cicero distinguished between affliction, worry, and anxiety, calling them disorders. He differentiated sadness from anxiety and considered anxiety a medical illness. Seneca suggested the cure for anxiety was to focus on the present. Epicurus recommended getting rid of negative thoughts about the past and fears about the future (Crocq 2015).

Hippocrates' contemporary philosophers coined the term "hysteria" meaning "of the uterus" (the root of "hysterectomy" and "hysterical") as they believed that such strong fearful emotions only happened in women. Plato believed that a woman's uterus was some kind of magical creature that roamed around the body causing all sorts of havoc, both psychological and physical. It was not until the 1600s that Willis theorized hysteria was a disorder of the brain.

Much later in history, and in the new world, hysterical women were often thought to be witches and they were drowned or burned at the stake. Sooner or later, in the age of Queen Victoria, hysterical women were considered "insane" and were often shipped off to asylums where they lived out the rest of their lives. The only therapy they received was electroshock, which may have appeared to cure their panic because it put them into a zombie-like state. Asylums were terrifying places in and of themselves where people were often chained up and left in filthy conditions with insufficient food or water. We can now only imagine how much worse such treatment would have made anyone's mental illness.

Boissier de Sauvages published, in 1763, a nosology for diseases. He described an anxiety disorder called panophobia. It was a terror without an obvious cause. Originally, it was considered nocturnal but then evolved into various subtypes (Crocq 2015).

During the American Civil War many solders or veterans were said to have had "irritable heart syndrome" or "nerve weakness" which, when examined closely through historical documents, was most certainly what we once called "shell shock" and now refer to as PTSD. Apparently, it was treated with opium which sounds a lot more fun than the treatment women got for anxiety.

Around the turn of the 19th century, a French physician named Philippe Pinel advocated for a more humane treatment of the mentally ill which became known as "moral therapy." Finally, someone had figured out that each mentally ill person was an individual and that if you removed their chains and simply talked to them, they might be helped. In America, treatment of the mentally ill with humane measures was championed by Dorothea Dix, a contemporary of Pinel.

By the early 20th century in America, not much had changed despite the progressive efforts of physicians such as Pinel and Dix. Of course, the dawn of the 20th century brought with it Sigmund Freud and the psychoanalysis movement which included Carl Jung and G. Stanley Hall. It was at this same time that hypnosis was being used as a form of treatment for "hysteria." Later, free association was employed to treat it, with or without a hypnotic state. The analysis of dreams came into popular usage to treat anxiety at this time as well.

It was not until the 1950s and 60s that actual reforms were made to improve conditions in mental hospitals. By this time, medications such as lithium and others had been developed, mainly to treat psychoses. It is worth noting that this is the period when we authors were born, so it really hasn't been long.

## Behavioral Therapy

As an alternative that challenged the pre-eminence of psychoanalysis, behaviorism emerged. Behaviorism examines the role of learning in human behavior. Finally, we begin to find among researchers and practitioners a foretaste of modern anxiety treatment. Championed by John B. Watson, Ivan Pavlov, and others, the ideas of classical conditioning morphed into the study of behaviorism with B.F. Skinner.

Most of us know and associate Pavlov with "classical conditioning." He conducted experiments in 1897 with dogs, where he paired a bell sound with offering food to the dog. He discovered that a conditioned stimulus (food) evoked a conditioned response (drooling). However, when he rang the bell without offering the food, he soon confirmed his hypothesis that the unconditioned stimulus also evoked the conditioned response.

Operant conditioning, first introduced by B.F. Skinner, is a learning method that employs rewards and punishments for behavior. Skinner believed that behavior is modified based on anticipating the reward or fearing the punishment.

In South Africa in the late 1950s, Joseph Wolpe developed systematic desensitization to treat anxiety (fear), using primarily animal research. The idea was that one could not be both terrified and calm at the same time. Patients were taught calming breathing techniques and progressive muscle relaxation exercises. Then, when confronted with the stimulus via exposure, they were encouraged to use breathing and relaxation to calm down. This method of exposure was popular as late as the 1980s, and many clinicians still employ it today. Its use did begin to decline as researchers—such as Philips (1985) for emetophobia and others who studied OCD and various anxiety disorders—noted that the fear or phobia tended to return after a time.

## Cognitive Therapy

Cognitive therapy began properly with the work of Alfred Adler and his education theory of how mistakes can cause behavioral problems in the future. Albert Ellis is said to have been influenced by Adler when he developed the initial method of cognitive-based therapy. However, the clinician most closely associated with cognitive therapy is Aaron Beck. Beck discovered that people who suffer from depression were found to have automatic negative thoughts, particularly about themselves but also about other people and the world in general. He eventually extended this theory to include people with anxiety as well. Beck called these automatic thoughts "core beliefs." These beliefs consist of thoughts about being worthless, incompetent, helpless, etc. To treat people with depression, Beck advocated for helping the patient to see and discover that their negative thoughts are flawed.

Beck was the grand master when it came to cognitive therapy, and it is difficult to imitate him. We have found that people with emetophobia, for the most part, know that their beliefs about vomiting being dangerous or harmful are mistaken. However, there are some people with emetophobia to whom I (Anna) have spoken online who have literally argued with me that vomiting is indeed dangerous and that you can most certainly "choke and die" from it. This is empirically untrue. Only someone *unconscious* and lying on their back can choke and die from vomiting. However, we as clinicians need to use great caution that we don't just spend 50 minutes arguing with our patients about the things they believe and hold dear to their hearts. There are exercises in cognitive therapy which can be very helpful for these patients, such as seeking evidence for one's beliefs and judging for oneself whether these beliefs would hold up in a court of law. We believe that cognitive therapy, or aspects of it, may be helpful for people with emetophobia, but only if they are low on the Emet-OCD continuum.

## Flooding

Flooding, as an anxiety treatment, came into vogue in the 1970s. It is a treatment wherein the patient is exposed to the feared stimulus for extended times. It is the goal of the "therapist to attain a maximal level of anxiety evocation from the patient" (Stampfl and Levis 1967, p. 500). For example, a person who fears dogs would be placed in a room with a dog until they cycled through panic and ultimately calmed down. Wijesinghe (1974) describes a case of one woman with emetophobia gradually taking more and more syrup of ipecac, becoming quite nauseous and finally vomiting. According to this single case study the woman no longer had a phobia of vomiting a year later. The study has never been replicated, and we daresay it would be difficult to find a large sample number of people with emetophobia willing to try it. In our extensive clinical experience as well as speaking to thousands of people with emetophobia online, vomiting may help patients for a short time, even a week or two, but then the phobia returns. A story that circulates in the online emetophobic community (although we have not been able to verify it) is of one woman with emetophobia who took ipecac and was so anxious she *couldn't* vomit, no matter what she did. To make matters worse, she was in a therapy appointment at the time and after two hours the therapist just sent her home, having gone way over her time. Since ipecac is in fact a type of poison, this woman was in more trouble than either she or her therapist realized. Without vomiting, ipecac can cause heart failure, brain damage, and even death. She was rushed to hospital and had her stomach pumped full of activated charcoal and then pumped out with a tube. She was very very sick and nearly didn't pull through. Take a wild guess as to whether she ended up more fearful or less fearful of vomiting after that.

There are a few things that make compelling, encouraging, or even suggesting a patient vomit a bad idea:

1. It's tricky to orchestrate.

2. It's unethical, violating the first principle of care: "do no harm."
3. It's cruel.
4. It doesn't work.
5. It could be dangerous.

I can't imagine either we or you could make it past point one and figure out how to make something like this happen anyway. Sometimes it may be possible to put a patient in the presence of someone vomiting, but it's unlikely it would be contagious. Patients can make themselves vomit by taking ipecac or some other vile substance, but this can go terribly wrong.

While it's true that most physicians don't swear the Hippocratic Oath anymore, and many of us are not physicians, we should still think long and hard about its underlying principle of "first, do no harm." Making someone sick, while they're at the same time terrified, seems to us to be unethical, and "encouraging" patients to do so when they are desperate for help is equally problematic.

We believe it is also cruel to flood a patient with fear. Olatunji, Deacon, and Abramowitz (2009) posed the question "The cruelest cure?" and explored ethical issues with exposure therapy. They did raise valid concerns about the training of clinicians in exposure therapy and the creation of safe environments or relationships. Ultimately, however, they concluded it is *not* cruel since exposure is the only evidence-based way out of an anxiety disorder, and anxiety even at high levels isn't harmful. Nevertheless, from having experienced that fear, I (Anna) can say with all professional confidence that it is the very height of cruelty to expose someone to the level of panic that most of the rest of humanity only feels when their life is at risk. The chances of that patient stopping the exposure before anxiety goes down also puts them at risk of being re-traumatized by it. These are all moot points because very few people with emetophobia would ever agree to participate in the kind of exposure that is flooding.

Maack, Deacon, and Zhao (2013) conducted a study with what they describe as "exposure therapy" with one woman with emetophobia. Their idea of exposure therapy was to begin with having the patient watch videos of vomiting, then meet the clinician at a restaurant and overeat, and in the penultimate session watch two clinicians vomit after a big breakfast. She was then instructed to try vomiting by gagging herself, but she was unable to do it. She also had been advised to eat a large breakfast before that session but hadn't done so. She was told that "the only step remaining... was for her to vomit and if she were unwilling to do so, it would not make sense to continue with exposures that were no longer creating distress" (p. 532). The clinician sent her home to practice vomiting with just water and to come back after eating bacon, eggs, hash browns, and orange juice to vomit something "chunkier" at the next session. Before that session, the patient called and said that she had practiced vomiting at home, understood it was no longer dangerous, and that she no longer needed treatment. She was contacted to fill out post-treatment assessments through which the researchers concluded that her fears about vomiting had subsided, and she no longer had a diagnosable phobia. She also told them at a three-year follow-up phone call that she was still phobia-free.

We are very suspicious of these findings. I (Anna) know how terrifying it is to have emetophobia and I think even a saint would not be truthful when they are as frightened as someone with emetophobia can be. I have had more than one patient tell me that they flat-out lied to previous therapists or to those running anxiety programs who wanted them to vomit. I have even seen reports issued by anxiety treatment programs that declared the patient "cured" of their phobia when they were sitting right in front of me, still terrified. The clinician in Maack et al. (2013) basically told the patient that there was no point in continuing with therapy unless she agreed to eat a large meal and vomit. We can't imagine what this would do to the therapeutic alliance if there ever was one. Unfortunately, the emetophobic community has also heard vicariously that this is what "exposure therapy" means and so they do not seek out treatment in the first place. We have heard many a sigh of relief when we explain that exposure therapy does not mean vomiting.

Riddle-Walker et al. (2016) note that attempts to self-induce vomiting typically reinforce the phobia, cannot be easily or healthily repeated, and may cause medical conditions. Keyes and Veale (2021, p. 59), the leading researchers on emetophobia, write: "We never make a person with emetophobia vomit on purpose. This is not likely to reduce anxiety and is not thought to be helpful or necessary."

Some patients may vomit *at the end of therapy*, either by chance or by their own choice, and if they do it tends to be helpful, although this would not be considered flooding. If vomiting occurs after sufficient therapy, it's as though everything they learned just clicks into place in their brain. But without proper therapy to give context, patients can and do get worse. In conclusion, flooding may work for a serious condition such as emetophobia, but it may also go terribly and irreversibly wrong. We also believe only the most courageous and, sadly, desperate patients would agree to try it, and so for all these reasons we firmly recommend against it. The risk of even asking is that it may send patients running from your office never to return to you, or potentially anyone else, ever again.

## Cognitive Behavioral Therapy (CBT)

The behaviorists had discovered that operant conditioning provided a helpful model in treating anxiety and phobias. As cognitive therapy began to become more popular, clinicians started to incorporate one modality with the other to successfully treat anxiety. Both schools of thought are concerned with what is happening to the patient at the present time, as opposed to the earlier analytic therapies which were and are primarily concerned with what happened to a person in the past, particularly in childhood.

CBT has become an effective way of treating emetophobia because no matter how the patient came to have the disorder, the treatment is the same. While many patients may have had different therapy modalities before that concentrated on their childhood, inner child, trauma, etc., nevertheless in a large majority of cases the only path out of emetophobia (that we know of so far) is through CBT with exposure and response prevention (ERP). However, it must be carried out in a particular way for clinicians to ensure maximum effectiveness and minimal distress and dropouts.

CBT literally sets itself up as an educational program, teaching the patient to become their own therapist. Some of the notable features of CBT are as follows:

- evidence-based (over 2,000 studies have been conducted on CBT)
- emphasis on the present day

- importance of psychoeducation
- goal oriented and short term
- structured therapy sessions
- action plans or "homework" assignments
- recording of thoughts in upsetting situations
- learning to discern the difference between flawed thinking (cognitive distortions) and reality.

When it comes to treating anxiety, and particularly emetophobia, CBT can weigh heavily on the "cognitive" aspect of therapy. Many clinicians believe the "behavioral" aspect lies only in the assigning of homework exercises about negative thoughts, so that some do not do exposure with their patients, nor do they assign exposures for homework. Cognitive treatment alone, or any other more modern therapy modality without exposure, has not been found to work for patients with emetophobia at the time of writing.

I (Anna) knew that my avoidance behavior was indicative of flawed thinking. There was no rational, logical reason why I should fear someone vomiting. Now what? I'm still terrified. One "CBT" therapist I saw for a few sessions (who did not even mention exposure) said to me: "Well, when you're ready to get rid of your phobia give me a call."

## ANNA'S STORY—PART 6

In 1983 I was pregnant with my first baby. No morning sickness, but I figured I really needed to get over this phobia once and for all. I finally worked up the courage to tell my doctor about it, and he referred me to a psychiatrist who had heard of a study being done here in Vancouver with other people who had a fear of vomiting. I was blown away that there were people on this planet that had the same fear that I did.

I eagerly joined the study which was conducted by Dr H. Claire Philips (1985). It was one of the first studies ever done on emetophobia. One of the baseline tests was to see how long you could watch a video of someone vomiting. She reports in the article that "[one] subject had a panic attack after only 0.5 sec of exposure" (p. 46). That was yours truly. The worst of the worst. Freak among freaks. At least, that's what I told myself. I didn't understand how the others could stand to have that video turned on at all.

We learned breathing techniques and progressive muscle relaxation skills, and then went through exposure therapy with a video of someone pretending to vomit (although she told us the person was vomiting, but they just had their head in a trash can the whole time). Dr Philips also had us try to think differently about vomiting. I was more scared of the other people in the group, to be honest, but nevertheless the therapy was immensely helpful. I learned that vomiting was unlikely most of the time, and that my nausea feelings were anxiety, basically all the time. I also learned how to control my anxiety with my breath, and the relaxation of my body.

From that time on I did not really fear vomiting myself. I learned that my analysis of body sensations was part of my anxiety and was not indicative of impending vomit. I eventually stopped thinking about vomiting day in and day out. This was enough to get me through two more kids and to stumble through life as a congregational minister, although I still made my husband deal with the kids when they were sick, and I would not put myself in any situation where I was trapped with someone who might vomit. The fear of someone else vomiting quickly returned, however, and became the most prominent manifestation of the phobia for me from that point on . The Disneyland trip, described in Chapter 1, was 13 years after I went through this group therapy.

---

Dattilio (2003) conducted a single-case experiment with a woman with emetophobia using gradual desensitization to the feeling of nausea. After clearing the experiment with numerous physicians and obtaining informed consent from the patient, he used a gradual increase in levels of syrup of ipecac to induce nausea, but not cause the patient to vomit. At the same time, similar to Philips (1985), he coached the patient on slow breathing techniques and progressive muscle relaxation as well as imagining a peaceful scene. Interestingly, the examiner mixed the ipecac with water and eventually gave the subject almost no ipecac at all, yet her anxiety and "nausea" still became elevated. Eventually the subject resolved her emetophobia and was still symptom-free at a two-year follow-up. Dattilio remarked in his conclusion that this was a complicated case with a complicated treatment and probably would not generalize to all people with emetophobia.

## Exposure and Response Prevention (ERP)

When it comes to treating OCD and anxiety disorders including phobias, an integral part of CBT is ERP. As we mentioned earlier, some clinicians are reluctant to use ERP, either because the patient is resistant to or does not fully understand the idea, or because the clinician thinks that exposure may be "too difficult" for them and that they "would not be able to handle it." It is also possible that some clinicians don't know how to structure ERP for emetophobia.

Exposure therapy, simply put, is exposing the patient to the feared stimulus, and having them remain there with the anxiety. This normally raises their subjective units of distress, depending on how frightening the patient perceives the stimulus. The idea is that the patient will enter the fearful situation without there being the consequence that they expect. For example, a patient may be encouraged to eat dessert after dinner wherein they will feel full and realize they did not vomit. Theoretically, this would lead the patient to learn that dessert is not "dangerous" after all and does not lead to vomiting. Unfortunately, many patients with emetophobia believe that they "just got lucky that one time" with the dessert, and the next time they might well vomit. This is why exposures require repetition.

Response prevention in the treatment of emetophobia means that the patient agrees not to use a safety behavior to cope with the exposure or, as is similar with OCD patients, not to perform a ritual to prevent vomiting. They *prevent* themselves from their normal anxious *response*. People with emetophobia have many safety behaviors which we listed in Chapter 1.

## Foa and Emotional Processing Theory (EPT)

Edna Foa has been highly influential in her research and teaching on the nature and treatment of anxiety disorders. Her research mainly focused on PTSD and OCD. EPT is "the modification of memory structures that underlie emotions" (Lovitz and Yusko 2021, p. 92). According to Foa, memories store three kinds of information: details of what we fear (*stimulus* information), ways to react to what we fear (*response* information), and meanings associated with what we fear (*meaning* information). Once this information is entrenched it is difficult to change. Foa and Kozak's

(1986) emotional processing theory states that to treat an anxiety disorder, first the emotional (memory) structure must be activated—so for anxiety disorders and OCD, there must be sufficient exposure to make the patient anxious. Second, there must be new information available to the patient which contradicts the previous (anxious) emotional structure. This is how new learning takes place.

For most people with emetophobia, the meaning in the emotional structure which gets reinforced time and time again is that vomiting is 100 percent horrific and terrible; a catastrophe of monumental scope; a disaster; one's worst nightmare; worse than death, and so on. The *stimulus* of body sensations, someone else vomiting, or feeling ill triggers the *response* of fight-or-flight (from nervousness to pure panic), the patient flees with avoidance or a safety behavior, and the *meaning* that is reinforced is that vomiting is dangerous and therefore it's a good thing they avoided it. Foa found over time that for a patient with anxiety to recover, they had to have an interruption in some aspect of the emotional structure so that new learning could occur.

David Yusko, who studied under Foa, writes about his patient with emetophobia and co-author Dara Lovitz: "Dara [needed] to learn that, although vomit may be gross, disgusting, and anxiety-provoking, she doesn't have to avoid it or protect herself from it in order to feel safe or know that she can handle or tolerate those emotions" (Lovitz and Yusko 2021, p. 95).

Yusko agrees with us that exposures, especially for emetophobia, must stimulate an anxiety response but they can't be so difficult that they overwhelm the patient or new learning cannot occur. We have found in our clinical practice that if someone is early or midway through the exposure process, and randomly gets norovirus and vomits, that this tends to reinforce the "vomiting is the worst thing ever" learning rather than "vomiting is not dangerous and although no one likes it, I can cope with it" learning. This makes our job more difficult, but still not impossible. I (Anna) once had a patient for whom this exact thing happened. Just when I thought all was lost, she said to me one day, "I guess the really worst [sic] thing that day was how terrified I was." I was shocked at her insight, but it turned the treatment process around to the right direction again.

## Craske and Inhibitory Learning

Michelle Craske and colleagues' research on anxiety disorders and their treatment has been paradigm shifting. She has published over 500 peer-reviewed journal articles as well as a number of self-help and other books on the subject. It is important to note that Craske's research has been mainly on people with OCD, panic disorder, social phobia, and GAD. Her work on specific phobias has focused on spider phobia, agoraphobia, and claustrophobia. Despite the differences between most of these disorders and emetophobia, Craske's work has merit for us and has informed our protocols for treating emetophobia. Craske's theory includes the following seven aspects (Craske 1999):

### Inhibitory Learning

Craske et al. (2014) became concerned that many people treated for their anxiety disorders relapsed, especially when they "naturally" avoided the feared stimulus. Let us say, for example, that someone is afraid of speaking in public and they go through 10–12 sessions where they gradually expose themselves to longer and longer times of speaking in public. Their fear becomes extinguished by the end but then they have no occasion to speak in public until five years later when they're asked to give a speech. They are greatly disheartened to learn that their fear has returned. This is of particular concern to us treating emetophobia because, no matter what we do, many adults might naturally only vomit once in 10 or 20 years. Even one year is a long time to (naturally or otherwise) avoid something once feared.

In Craske's inhibitory learning model, the original fear structure or learning is not replaced during the process of ERP. Rather, the original fear structure is left intact, and a new secondary structure is learned that has the function of inhibiting the original fear structure. Both structures exist according to this model. The model also explains some of the problems not explained by the emotional processing model such as the spontaneous recovery of the fear when there is a long time from the last exposure, the context changing from what is treated, or adverse experiences following treatment.

Craske, and other of her contemporaries, discovered that habituation alone isn't enough to successfully treat a phobia. ERP needs to teach the patient new information which *inhibits* or blocks out the original fear. Inhibitory learning focuses on *tolerating* anxiety rather than trying to eliminate it. It teaches the patient that anxiety is safe and tolerable, so avoidance and safety behaviors are not necessary.

## Expectancy Violation

The greater the mismatch between the expectation for the exposure relative to the outcome (actual experience), the stronger the inhibitory learning. The exposure is designed to teach someone what they need to learn rather than reduce or control their fear. For example, for a person with emetophobia, the expected outcome is that the exposure will lead to vomiting. The exposure needs to take place until that expectation is "violated." Learning takes place when the negatively expected outcome does or doesn't take place or wasn't as bad as anticipated, not whether the fear is diminished.

## Response Prevention

Removal of safety behaviors is crucial for the treatment. Although safety behaviors reduce distress in the short term, they interfere with inhibitory learning. It is important to phase these out during treatment.

## Variability

Cues that trigger anxiety are going to vary in life. Variability during treatment more closely resembles actual experience and should be incorporated to improve inhibitory learning during treatment. Changing the triggers, the level of intensity, or items out of order in the hierarchy can enhance this learning.

## Multiple Contexts

Similar to variability, changing contexts of the exposures in various ways like being alone, different locations, various times during the day, before and after eating, and whether the exposure is imaginal or in real life can enhance inhibitory learning.

## Affect Labeling

Having patients state their emotional response without trying to change it during the exposure process also promotes inhibitory learning. Foa and Kozak (1986) hypothesized that if the patient used distraction when they encounter the phobic stimulus in vivo, or during

ERP, it would interfere with successful emotional processing. Craske et al. (1991) went on to discover that if patients were asked to give details of the feared object they were encountering in the exposure, and name the emotions they were feeling, that their anxiety was higher. Distraction has since been seen as a form of avoidance in anxiety disorders.

### Deepened Extinction

Deepened extinction is the result of combining multiple cues or triggers during an exposure. So, with emetophobia, one might try an interoceptive exposure such as spinning around to become dizzy with the sounds of vomiting in the background, or even a video playing. It's also a good idea to eventually try to do any one or two of the exposure elements first with a full stomach after a big meal, and later when one feels actually nauseous. More of implementing this methodology will be discussed in Chapter 6.

## Acceptance and Commitment Therapy (ACT)

ACT is part of what is known as the "third wave" of CBT and is immensely popular within the psychotherapeutic community at the time of writing. While we applaud the modality and the subsequent research on it that has been undertaken, we also want to begin with a word of caution when using solely an ACT approach to treat emetophobia.

ACT was developed by Steven C. Hayes in the early 1980s. Its objective is not to eliminate difficult feelings, but rather to accept them and commit to living one's life toward one's values and goals. Thoughts, feelings, and sensations (including anxiety) are described as "private events." ACT teaches people to "just notice" these private events, *accept* and even embrace them. If one's private event is anxiety, therefore, they should not try to control their anxiety but rather to notice it, tolerate it, and allow it to be there. The idea is that any attempt to control anxiety will necessarily result in the use of an avoidance or safety behavior. Things like slow, even breathing, and relaxing one's body are therefore seen as safety behaviors. ACT also encourages people to embrace their personal values and goals and to *commit* to work and reach for them, fully living life, despite whatever private events they encounter along the way. A single case study demonstrated that ACT could be effective for emetophobia (Bogusch, Moeller, and O'Brien 2018).

We believe that some components from ACT can and should be incorporated into treatment for emetophobia, but we don't believe that an ACT approach alone would be sufficient for success for most patients with emetophobia. Our treatment modality will be discussed at length in Chapter 6.

### Mindfulness

Mindfulness, or attention to the present moment, is included as a feature of ACT. Mindfulness can mean slightly different things to different people. Mindfulness is of particular importance in the treatment of emetophobia, as those with the disorder usually spend an inordinate amount of time thinking about and worrying about the future. By "future" we do not mean the plans or goals for living in the future but rather things like "what if I'm sick," "what if that chicken wasn't cooked," "what if my husband drinks too much," etc. Mindfulness would encourage patients to simply notice whatever feelings, thoughts, or sensations are present for them right now.

One part of mindfulness may be meditation. This sometimes takes the form of just sitting quietly and focusing on the here and now. It could also be listening to sounds of falling rain, waves on the beach or soft music. Another form of mindfulness meditation is guided imagery, either incorporating progressive muscle relaxation or on its own.

## Third-Wave CBT Treatments and Emetophobia

We must use caution, as treatment modalities such as inhibitory learning, emotional processing theory, and ACT have not been fully researched or tested with emetophobia. Almost all the research done with all of these modalities was done with OCD, PTSD, or phobias with a limited and definable stimulus such as spiders, agoraphobia, or claustrophobia.

For a long time, I (Anna) had a lot of trouble with the concept of "just noticing" anxiety without trying to control it. Imagine if my husband had come up the cliff on our way back from Disneyland and told me to "just notice" my anxiety. How in the world could I *not* notice it? I have since understood, however, that sometimes our anxiety is indeed not noticeable and yet it pushes us to do or avoid certain behaviors. Nevertheless, I still do not teach my patients to "notice" their anxiety lest it sound ridiculous or condescending, but rather to "take note of it," meaning note what it is from 0–10. This is much more concrete and makes sense no matter how high the anxiety is. A family member or support person can also ask this question if the patient's anxiety is so high that they cannot think clearly.

### Variability of Exposures

We do *not* recommend telling patients that the exposure process will be anything but carefully structured, one step at a time. In fact, we promise patients that there will be *no* surprises during exposure exercises. We promise this because to do otherwise would probably impact a patients' willingness to do exposure in the first place. We always describe the exposure (pictures or videos) to the patient and ask for their consent before showing it to them. Once they've gone through all the pictures, videos, and sounds, we have adults do their own Google or YouTube search for pictures and videos to meet the requirement of variability. We have yet to work with anyone who was not willing to do this by the time we arrived at this level.

### ACT and Emetophobia

People with emetophobia normally have goals of having children, traveling, or holding down a job. They value time with family members and friends, and the ability to freely go wherever they desire. Emetophobia makes these goals impossible to achieve for many people, so incorporating the principles of ACT along with exposure therapy can be extremely helpful. The clinician must use caution, however, at least at first, with using words like "acceptance" and "commitment" as they each come with possible triggers. Since emetophobia almost always presents as very severe, the idea that the patient needs to "accept" just about anything about the condition can lead to hopelessness and despair. Who would want to accept having debilitating panic attacks, sometimes daily, where you feel as if you are dying? Many patients at first cannot even accept that they will vomit someday, even though this is also true. We as clinicians know that this is not what Hayes and others who employ ACT meant by the term. We always give our patients hope that if they can begin to accept and tolerate feelings of anxiety at least from 1–8 out of 10 that eventually the anxiety will not bother showing up anymore. At the very least it won't show up at panic-attack levels. I (Anna) often tell patients it's like your amygdala is saying: "Well, she's not doing anything. She's just sitting there. So I guess it can't be dangerous after all." Acceptance and tolerance of anxiety can and will lead to more of an anxiety-free life such as that which I now enjoy.

The term "commitment" is less of a hot button, but it could come across as condescending to some patients. I have so many memories of therapists telling me that I *just needed to commit* to (facing my fears, for example) or that I wasn't willing to make the commitment to getting better (by doing the impossible exposure tasks they suggested). Lack of acceptance of something is not nearly as pejorative a term as lack of commitment.

Once patients understand that the principles of ACT are that one commits to one's values in life, then it is a bit easier to swallow. I don't bother much with the word; however, thanks to ACT, I do encourage my patients to begin living their lives and reaching for their goals despite their anxiety going to moderately high levels, and that this is the road to recovery.

## Christie-Russ on Emetophobia Treatment

As you will have gleaned by now, we are well-versed in anxiety treatment theory and research. Partly this is because we have been searching, pondering, and working out how to treat emetophobia either for ourselves (in Anna's case) or for someone close to us (in David's case), and ultimately for our patients and for yours. As such we have read dozens of books, hundreds of articles and spent thousands of hours "listening and talking" to people with emetophobia in online forums as well as working with over 300 of our own patients. Nevertheless, we are clinicians and not researchers, physicians, or theorists. We have, however—and now present to you, our colleagues—our own theory of treatment for emetophobia.

Our theory, which is neither new nor radical, is based on the following three factors:

1. Severity: Unlike many other anxiety disorders, especially

phobias, emetophobia almost universally presents as very severe. We have illustrated this briefly in previous chapters with Anna's story of her trip to Disneyland. Emetophobia is not just being grossed out by or not liking to vomit. It is wholly debilitating, ruining the lives of those who suffer from it.

2. The nausea/anxiety loop: Unlike a phobia of spiders, heights, or cats, increased anxiety causes increased nausea *which in turn causes increased anxiety*. In spider phobia, when the patient's anxiety rises they may experience some nausea, but they won't care because that is not what scares them. People with emetophobia, if encouraged to allow anxiety to rise to high levels, will naturally experience nausea (because digestion slows or shuts down with the sympathetic nervous system response), and this will confirm to the person with emetophobia that they are indeed sick, making it even more difficult for them to tolerate and less likely to continue with the exposure.

3. Idiosyncrasies: Some people with emetophobia have troubling memories of vomiting; some have none. Some have histories of trauma; some do not. Some have constant nausea; some do not. Some are "high OCD"; some are low. Some are very courageous; some are not. Some come from lovely families; some do not. Some fear only seeing/hearing others vomit; most fear themselves only; some fear others if they have something contagious; some don't care. Some only panic instantly; some have slow rising anxiety. Some have comorbidities; some do not. Some have medical conditions; some do not. Some are very young children; some are angry teenagers; some are fed-up adults. In whatever way the person presents with emetophobia, we can guarantee that their problem is a complex combination of any of the above, and so must be treated with great compassion, attention to detail, and the utmost of care and respect.

## Treatment Theory for Emetophobia

With almost all our patients, we combine the earlier theory and practice of gradual desensitization with "third wave" CBT theories. It breaks down into these five simple points:

1. *ERP:* We employ ERP with virtual, in vivo and interoceptive exposures and the giving up of safety behaviors. With *low OCD* patients (Figure 2.1 in Chapter 2), we also employ cognitive restructuring strategies.
2. *PMR:* We teach progressive muscle relaxation and slow breathing techniques for patients to use *only when anxiety is at panic-attack levels.*
3. *Acceptance:* We coach patients to accept and learn to tolerate anxiety *as long as they are not panicking.*
4. *Trigger words:* We are careful, especially at first, with the use of words and phrases such as "tolerate," "acceptance," "commitment," "control," and trigger words about vomit.
5. *Controlling anxiety:* We are okay with patients looking upon their anxiety as something negative, and we teach them both how to control it and when not to control it.

## Conclusion

The treatment of anxiety disorders has come a long way since boring holes in our skulls and burning witches at the stake. We are deeply indebted to those early scholars who showed us how research on conditioning could eventually be used to treat phobias. The work of Foa, Craske, Hayes, and many others in what is known as the "third wave" of CBT has added to our understanding of how phobias work, and what might be done to structure treatment for them.

We are also grateful for the handful of scholars and experts who have researched emetophobia, and for those authors such as Keyes and Veale, Yusko and Lovitz, and Ken Goodman who have published excellent self-help books for people with emetophobia in just the past two years. Russ and McCarthy's (2010) *Turnaround: Turning Fear into Freedom* and *Emetophobia Supplement* (2016) for children is an excellent self-help tool for parents of children with emetophobia. The efficacy of the Turnaround program has been established by a randomized controlled trial (Infantino, Donovan, and March 2016).

With this history and research in mind, we now turn our attention to the treatment of emetophobia.

— *Chapter 5* —

# PSYCHOEDUCATION

Psychoeducation is an important aspect of all CBT, and this could not be truer than with emetophobia. This chapter will give clinicians a complete description of each aspect of psychoeducation that we undertake with patients with emetophobia before beginning treatment. People with emetophobia will have mustered up a great deal of courage just to come to a clinician in the first place and tell them their story and the many ways in which emetophobia has affected their lives. For these patients to give informed consent for exposure therapy they must understand exactly how it works, why it works, and what is expected of them in order for it to work. It is common for us to have to cover aspects of psychoeducation multiple times during the course of treatment.

Clinicians are encouraged to take from this chapter any or all of the wording that they wish. The chapter is duplicated in handout form on our website[1] for you to copy and use with your patients as you wish (scan the QR code below).

---

1    www.emetophobia.net/exposure/psychoeducation-adults

## No Vomiting

The first and most important part of psychoeducation for people with emetophobia is to reassure them that you will not make them vomit or ask them to make themselves vomit. Vomiting is not part of exposure therapy because the problem is not vomiting; it is anxiety. Treatment with exposures will focus on slowly raising their anxiety to about mid-level and learning to recognize, assess, and tolerate the feeling without using a safety behavior or any attempt to calm down.

## Exposure

For most patients, the thought of exposure is terrifying. I (David) like to joke with my patients, "I am going to make you anxious on purpose and you have to pay me for it. What could be wrong with that?" That usually warrants a smile, but the idea is still hard to wrap one's head around. Knowing that it works is helpful to a point and is an important part of the psychoeducational aspect of treatment.

We explain that exposure therapy means beginning with very simple, easy things like words or phrases, followed by drawings, cartoons, pictures of nauseous people, and so on. The idea is that they will allow their anxiety to rise, but never to the level of panic, and they will do nothing to try to control or lower their anxiety. Things like breathing slowly or relaxing muscles or telling yourself things like "I won't vomit" are actually safety behaviors when used in this context and they will not be needed because we will not show them anything that makes them panic.

The idea of not controlling anxiety may be foreign to your patients who have read of desensitization online or had other clinicians coach them to do so. You can remind them that despite trying to breathe and relax, their phobia remains, or they wouldn't be here.

In addition to explaining how exposure works, we like to remind patients that they are already thinking and feeling distress about what they fear *all the time*. We are not asking anyone to do anything that isn't already happening. We are just going to do what their brain is doing with a plan to make it less scary. Their nervous system is already forcing exposure in an attempt to overcome the fear. We tell patients we are just going to help their brain finish what it is trying to do and stop the things that are keeping that from working.

## No Surprises

It is important to tell patients that we will not surprise them. We will describe the exposure in as much detail as possible, and then ask permission to continue before showing them the image or starting the video. We let them know that it is important to give us feedback if they do not want to do something or if they need more time. One way I (David) express it is, "I don't worry about something you can't do at the moment; let's just find something in that direction and do that." Rather than think of this particular exposure as an either/or, think of it as a continuum. Many patients, if they are not able to do something, are tempted to quit that step. We really work at helping them creatively think about how to break the step down into smaller steps. We also encourage the caregiver(s) (or partner if treating an adult) to make sure the family doesn't think it is fun to surprise the patient.

## Terminology Used

I (David) tell patients that I will not use any words or explicit descriptions, as far as possible, until I have a better idea of what might be triggering. Of course, in the process of getting a history, there will likely be things that are triggering. I also listen very carefully to how they might describe what happened and try to use their own expressions as we talk. I will still avoid using any explicit words if possible. I will often use an expression like "the thing" or similar. It is interesting that the exact same description or words can be much more triggering if used by someone else. I (Anna) mainly work with adults. I use the word "vomit" right from the beginning, regardless of what term they use. I like for people to get used to the sound of it. When I work with children, I approach the work as David describes above.

## ANNA'S STORY—PART 7

One month after we got back from Disneyland, I was diagnosed with breast cancer. Just when I thought my worst nightmare was on that California roadway. All the things I was the most terrified of: general anesthetic, chemotherapy, being pinned down for radiation treatments. But what was the alternative? Die a horrible death and leave my three kids without a mother? No, one of the reasons we have this phobia is that our survival instinct is hyper-aware and trigger-happy. When it really smacks you in the face, you'll choose to live. And yes, just like other people with emetophobia, I had said a thousand times with conviction that I would rather die than vomit, and definitely I would rather die than have chemo.

I didn't vomit after surgery, and chemo wasn't as bad for me as everyone on TV had made it out to be. They gave me good drugs like ondansetron, and I was a little nauseous for a day, but the chemo didn't make me vomit. However, at the end of the last chemo treatment I got a severe and annoying abscess. The doctor prescribed me an antibiotic without thinking that I'd just had chemo and wouldn't be able to digest said antibiotic. I knew for about an hour that I was going to vomit. I could just tell. I paced back and forth and tried to clench my entire GI tract together so it wouldn't happen, but finally it did anyway. I'll never forget the words that entered my head immediately afterward: "Well that was a big fat nothing." My next thought was, "I can't believe I wasted all that time being scared of that big fat nothing."

## The Patient Is in Control

With exposure therapy, the patient is in control of the entire course of treatment. Before we do an exposure together they will be fully informed about what they are about to see, and then *they* will make the decision as to whether they see it or not. If they cannot do the exposure, or cannot do it today, there will be no judgment on your part. It is on *you* to find something easier for them to do instead. They may also use the rest of the session to talk or do anything else that they feel would be helpful.

## Goal-Setting

As with all CBT treatment, setting goals for oneself is an important way to measure success in therapy. Setting goals will help to point the patient in a different direction than avoidance of vomiting.

Of course, everyone has the goal of "not having emetophobia anymore." We understand that. But usually, it's best to come up with some goals that are more specific and measurable. Some of the goals our patients have come up with over the years are:

- getting pregnant or having children
- traveling
- going ahead with a surgery or medical procedure
- getting on to or off anti-anxiety or other medications
- returning to school or work
- sending one's children to school, parties, sleepovers, or the playground
- eating out at a restaurant
- trying new foods
- going to someone else's house for a meal or overnight.

## The Importance of Homework

After each session homework will be assigned. This may be in the form of reading or listening to something about their treatment. It may also be practicing exposures that you have already done together in session or sending the patient out on their own for a "real life" exposure such as eating in a coffee shop or restaurant. You may assign giving up one or more safety behaviors. These homework assignments are not just important, they are *imperative* for your patient's treatment. In the end, the clinician is the guide, mentor, coach, teacher, and companion, showing the patient the way through this difficult path and journey to healing. Let the patient know that you are not responsible for their success or lack of it: they are. Success comes through doing the consistent completion of homework exercises. If your patient does not have the time or cannot make the time, then it would be best to delay treatment for their emetophobia until they do/can.

## Get Back on the Horse

For as long as humans can remember, "get back on the horse" has been the accepted treatment for fears. If you fall off a horse and don't get back on immediately, then at some point you will never get back on. I suppose today the equivalent might be "get back on the bike; back on the skateboard; back on the surfboard; back behind the wheel."

Anxiety and fear, regardless of how severe, is a universal experience. There are documented cases of "adrenalin junkies" who love to do dangerous things and find the rush of adrenalin and panic exhilarating.

These people are rare and many of them end up dead. But everyday people have everyday fears. If something is dangerous and hurts you, you'll naturally be afraid of it. Problems arise when you see something as dangerous that isn't. This is called a "perceived threat." Most people can tolerate this fear, and so they get back on the horse. Before long, they're riding again with no fear because falling off a horse and being critically injured or dying is rare.

Vomiting is one of those things in life that literally *everyone* hates. It kind of hurts. It feels gross. It tastes disgusting in your mouth, and it looks like the rotting vegetable soup they serve in hell. However, it isn't dangerous. It can't hurt you one bit and in fact it's meant to rid your body of poison or toxins from disease, so it actually helps you. Peter Silin, a now retired therapist, once said on one of my (Anna's) podcasts (Christie 2020a): "vomiting is your body's way of caring for you." I thought this was just a lovely way of looking at it. I tell my patients that vomiting is "normal, natural and neutral." It is normal because everyone does it. It's so easy a child can do it. It's natural because it is an automatic response that we don't have to think about to rid our body of toxins, much like urinating or defecating. We have little control over any of these bodily functions. We can feel them as imminent, and get to a bathroom, but we cannot put any of them off when they really need to happen. Vomiting is neutral because on the one hand it is nasty and no one likes it, but on the other hand it saves our lives.

## The SUD Scale

Throughout treatment, we have our patients use a scale from 0–10 to measure their anxiety and ensure that it is neither too high nor too low. SUD stands for "subjective units of distress." The key word is "subjective" which means that the number your patient gives cannot possibly be wrong, as it is their number and theirs alone. After a short time, we find our patients and ourselves become accustomed to the numbers they use and what they mean for them.

On the scale, 0 means no anxiety at all, and 10 means the worst panic possible. If you describe the scale to the patient in this manner, then they cannot give you a number like 11 or 1000, no matter how anxious they feel. We often ask our patients what the numbers mean for them in terms of body sensations. It is interesting to note that many of them cannot tell us what 10 feels like. We believe that is because phobias are *anticipatory anxiety* in general. Since the actual thing isn't dangerous, then if one's anxiety goes all the way to 10 (they vomit) their anxiety level usually goes right down. After all, they're still standing there, not dead and feeling fine.

We still will use SUD scores even though there is evidence that decreased anxiety isn't always the best framework. It just works clinically. SUD scores are practical.

## Disgust

Van Overveld et al. discovered in their (2008) survey of people with emetophobia and a non-emetophobic control group that the emetophobic group had a significantly higher level of disgust propensity and sensitivity. I (Anna) ask my patients if they have noticed that they find things disgusting in general when others do not. If they answer in the affirmative, I will mention the research on this subject and let them know that they are certainly not alone. I also tell them that the exposure therapy they're about to embark on will actually help with this, and that often medical students and student nurses have to do gradual exposure to disgusting things before they can continue their studies if they are particularly sensitive.

## The Brain Made Easy

As part of psychoeducation, I (Anna) used to take 10 or 15 minutes with each patient to give what I jokingly called the "two-dollar lecture" on how the brain works, in a simplified—*very* simplified—version. Here is basically what I say:

> The human brain is the most complicated, intricate, and fascinating entity in the known universe. Scientists have mapped much of the brain and know a lot about it, but there is still much that we do not understand and we don't know exactly how it works.

The brain is a bit like a bunch of organs all squished together. So, there are many different parts, all of which are complicated. The various parts work together as systems that do all the work of our brains.

But for today, I'm just going to divide the brain into three easy parts (see Figure 5.1).

The first part is the oldest from an evolutionary perspective. We're going to call that the *reptilian brain*. It is sort of at the back of your head, in the middle, at the top of your spinal cord. The second part is called the *midbrain*, and the newest part at the front (your forehead) is called the *neocortex* or "new brain" as it is newest from an evolutionary perspective. The neocortex is responsible for those functions that separate us from other mammals.

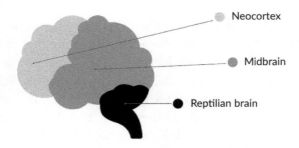

Neocortex

Midbrain

Reptilian brain

**FIGURE 5.1:** THE THREE-PART BRAIN

The midbrain is responsible for many things such as walking, talking, seeing, hearing, breathing, heart beating, emotions, music, art, envisioning, creativity, and so on. The neocortex is responsible for reason, logic, mathematics, organization, and what we call executive functions. As the brain is at the top of your spinal cord, changes in the brain are felt in or through the body, or they're carried out through the body. So, when the brain sends a signal, it's sending a signal to some other part of your body, and that part of your body is responding. It is as if the brain really looks like Figure 5.2, continuing down the spinal column and out to all your nerve endings.

Let's focus on that reptilian brain. It consists of a couple of parts, but the most important part for people with anxiety disorders is called the amygdala. It's the Latin word for "almonds" because the amygdala are two almond-shaped organs. The amygdala have one primary function: to keep you alive. What does a reptile need to know other than to kill something and eat it before it kills you and eats you? We also call this the "survival instinct." We use the word "instinct" because we don't have to think about it. Survival is an automatic response.

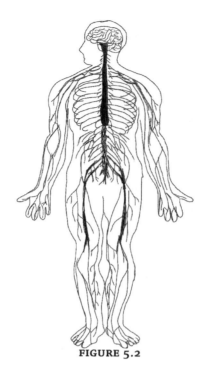

**FIGURE 5.2**

When triggered from a threat or perceived threat, our amygdala can only send out one message: "Danger! You're going to die!" It's a bit like sounding a fire alarm. When you hear it, you may freeze for a moment but if there's a bomb or a fire, then you will run like a cheetah. When the brain senses danger, I've heard that the amygdala can fire in 1/5000th of a second.[2] Or 5000 times per second. A thought takes at least one second, maybe two or three. Meanwhile you've been told 15,000 times that you're going to die. That's why phobias are really *really* scary.

The body's nervous system or system of nerves (as in Figure 5.2) at rest is called the "parasympathetic nervous system." This is a calm mental and emotional state where your heart is beating slowly but surely, your breathing is steady, and you haven't got a care in the world. Once the amygdala fires the danger signal, however, your brain

---

2   This may be an exaggeration. However, the amygdala are faster than a wild stallion, while one's thought process is a slow-but-steady mule.

automatically switches your body over to what is called the "sympathetic nervous system." Here is what goes on in your body when that happens:

1. An outpouring of adrenalin surges from your adrenal glands.
   a. At low levels adrenalin feels like "butterflies in the stomach."
   b. At higher levels people experience a "jolt" like electricity going through their body.
   c. At very high levels people have been known to gain super-human strength.
2. Heart rate increases.
3. Breathing becomes shallow and fast.
4. The body heats up.
5. Palms or other areas begin to sweat to release the heat.
6. Muscles tense, ready to run or fight.
7. Bowels loosen.
8. Digestion slows down or stops, causing nausea.

This sympathetic nervous system prepares you for "fight or flight." We now know that it also can make you "freeze" (which is usually temporary) or "fawn." Fawn is a newer insight which refers to the way in which people try to please a dangerous person or calm the situation down. It is most prominent in those with a history of parental abuse and currently experiencing domestic violence or chaotic situations. With emetophobia, one is most likely to flee; if someone tries to hold you back from fleeing, then you will fight. "Fight" may also describe an emotion of intense anger that people with emetophobia feel toward others, for example, if they come to work sick or put a vomit scene in their movie.

When the amygdala fires because of a *perceived* danger (like vomiting), the body reaction is exactly the same as if you see a grizzly bear coming at you. If someone else is ill, you will try to run away if you can or avoid going near them in the first place. This is the "flight" or fleeing reaction. If you feel nauseous yourself, you cannot run and you cannot fight. So, although you still get all these body reactions you will also get a marked feeling of doom. It's a catastrophic feeling like you're caught in the middle of a bloody murder scene. It's horror and terror with no way out. You may feel as if you cannot breathe.

You might think you're going crazy or you're literally dying. You aren't, but that's the feeling. You can get a pounding headache and even chest pain because of your heart thumping so hard. You can get very dizzy and lightheaded because the oxygen is needed more in your arms and legs for the running and fighting. Your vision could go blurry because clear vision is not as important since grizzly bears are blatantly and manifestly obvious. As a result of all these body sensations and feelings, you may get to the point where you feel almost like you're not in reality. I used to say I felt that I was swimming in a milkshake. Sometimes it is also described as tunnel vision. This non-reality feeling we call dissociation, derealization, or depersonalization.

Now, if you get all of these feelings at once, or any group of them to a very high degree, we call that a *panic attack*. And it feels awful. It won't hurt you, but that is how it feels. Panic attacks only last about 15–20 minutes unless you employ a safety behavior. Using a safety behavior means you think there is an actual danger, which maintains the alarm. People with emetophobia are very skilled at employing invisible safety behaviors like reassuring thoughts.

Your neocortex at the front of your brain *knows* there's no danger, but it has not yet *learned* it—which sounds silly but there is a clear difference. Besides, it's too late. Your body fully believes that there is a danger, and it is only acting accordingly and automatically. The learning must take place in a different way than simply having your emetophobia triggered and enduring or "white-knuckling" your way through the situation.

The good news is that it is possible for the front of your brain to talk to the back. But it must do so in a structured way so that slowly and carefully your amygdala and your body *learn* that the danger is not real. With exposure therapy done properly, we want to activate your amygdala just a bit, so you're feeling no more than maybe 5-out-of-10 afraid. And then you stay in the scary situation, for example, looking at a word or a drawing or a picture, until you can take note of, understand, and tolerate the fear, or until you no longer feel afraid. It's also important that you employ no safety behaviors while you're in the situation. Your amygdala will then learn that there's no danger because you've done nothing, and you're fine. As you've always *done something* to make yourself "safe" at least part of your brain believes that there *must* have been some danger and thank goodness you used that safety behavior, or you would have been eaten by a grizzly bear.

In your brain, for reasons we never really know, a superhighway was built from the stimulus—nausea or vomiting—to the amygdala response.

That superhighway will always be there; there's nothing we can do to remove it. However, with exposure and response prevention therapy we can build a new highway from the stimulus to a place of calm. The point is not eliminating the fear. The point is being able to tolerate the fear in many situations so that eventually it either stops showing up, or it shocks you for a moment, but you recover immediately.

I (Anna) consider myself completely phobia free. I avoid nothing; I have no safety behaviors. And I never think about vomiting outside of my work. But if someone vomits on TV, or right next to me, I'll jump about ten feet high on the inside (1/5000th of a second). But then I just take a breath in and I'm fine. I sometimes have to say to myself, "You're not afraid of that anymore," while breathing in, but that's it.

## Futility and Hope

**FIGURE 5.3:** THE ROAD TO RECOVERY

Figure 5.3 illustrates that the road to recovery from emetophobia is long, often uphill, and fraught with fear. However, the patient is already on that road. They are afraid most of the time. Their solution is to exit the road by avoiding what they fear or implementing a safety behavior, but this only takes them around in a circle and deposits them farther back on the road, still in fear. It may feel good momentarily when they are off the road, but it will take them back again and again in a never-ending roundabout of anxiety. And yet there is hope. Remaining on the road and plodding away, one step at a time, will get them to their destination. Hope is so very important for patients because their endless circle of futility and fear is such a hopeless existence. Even though emetophobia is a terribly debilitating condition, it is highly treatable. Thousands of clinicians are now treating emetophobia very successfully and tens of thousands of people with emetophobia are finding healing and a new lease on life. With commitment to the homework and the process, and just a touch of raw courage, every patient can succeed as well.

## Chapter 6

# TREATING ADULTS WITH EMETOPHOBIA

## Anna S. Christie

### Treatment Conceptualization

Research done by Orme, Challacombe, and Roxborough (2022) on two mothers with emetophobia who had small children is the first case study we have seen to use a treatment protocol based on current research. Both women made significant progress. Their treatment, after proper assessment using EMET-Q13, SPOVI, and two other measures, involved psychoeducation, cognitive restructuring, exposure through a hierarchy, imagery re-scripting, and relapse prevention.

Riddle-Walker et al. (2016) in a randomized controlled trial used 3–5 sessions to address flash-forwards (with imaginal exposure) and flashbacks (with imagery rescripting). Sessions 4–7 addressed dropping safety behaviors and the thoughts which contributed to the fear. Sessions 6–12 involved developing a hierarchy of fears, doing exposure in imagination, and finally exposures to pictures, sounds, and smells. Interoceptive exposure was used if appropriate and subjects were coached on relapse prevention.

Based on our theory outlined at the end of Chapter 4, I work with people with emetophobia in approximately 16–20 sessions using the following key elements of treatment:

1. assessment including empathic listening to the patient's story, questionnaires, and family history taking
2. goal setting

3.  psychoeducation
4.  giving up avoidance and safety behaviors
5.  cognitive restructuring, if appropriate
6.  teaching/encouraging proper breathing and progressive muscle relaxation (via YouTube videos)
7.  exposure through established online hierarchy (virtual and in vivo exposures)
8.  interoceptive exercises
9.  weekly homework:
    a.  review of in-session online exposures
    b.  work on avoidance and safety behaviors
    c.  in vivo exposures
10. ongoing encouragement of self-efficacy.

## Session Structure

I begin each session with three important questions:

1.  "How are you?" This question goes against everything I learned in therapist school and the advice of each of my supervisors. Perhaps it's the Canadian in me, but I think it shows that I care. Their answer is also the first thing I jot down in my notes. I read over those first lines before every session. It is amazing to see a patient go from "Okay I guess..." to "Pretty good" to "Good!"
2.  "Has anything challenged you emetophobia-wise this week?" We discuss the challenge, and how they handled it. We then talk about how they might have handled it differently. This is an opportunity for review and ongoing psychoeducation.
3.  "What have you been working on?" My supervisor always started every session with this question. Before long I thought about it and realized that I should actually always be working on something! This question leads into the homework debrief.

Discussion of the preceding three questions should take ten minutes but sometimes this extends to 20 which is fine occasionally. I spend the remaining 30 to (preferably) 40 minutes doing exposures with the patient.

## Hierarchy of Fears

In order to treat emetophobia with ERP it is important to have a hierarchy of fears from the least fearful to the most fearful thing. The "most fearful" is always vomiting, but we do not put that at the top of the hierarchy as vomiting is not important as a goal. I therefore have patients put "doing something where I'm at risk of vomiting" at the top of the hierarchy.

While Abramowitz, Deacon, and Whiteside (2019) suggest a list of fears in no particular order, rather than a gradual hierarchy, I have yet to find a patient who would agree to that arrangement in the beginning. However, although I do not advocate surprises at first, as patients are normally too anxious for that, once they have grown confident in their ability to tolerate triggers (about three-quarters of the way through treatment), I have them choose random videos of vomiting on YouTube. This enables us to walk the line between what works clinically (the patient's comfort) and the variability recommended by the theory of inhibitory learning. The list of sounds of vomiting that I use is also in no particular order.

I have worked with patients with emetophobia for the past 12 years and have saved us both a lot of time and hence the patient a lot of money by using the same hierarchy with everyone. I developed the hierarchy myself once I had enough material to put up on a free resource website. Over the years I have added and subtracted many items from the hierarchy but kept basically the same structure. At first, I put the trigger items in the order in which I thought appropriate. But I made changes based on feedback of the majority of people with emetophobia. For example, I found it easier to hear sounds of vomiting than to look at videos of people vomiting. However, after time, I found that nearly every patient experienced it the other way around. So, I changed the hierarchy to have videos come first and sounds later.

You can find this hierarchy to use on our website, or if you'd prefer to develop your own hierarchy with the patient, then the next easiest thing to do is to go over the table of contents of the hierarchy on our website[1] with them (scan the QR code on the following page).

---

1   www.emetophobia.net/exposure

## Safety Behaviors

In addition to the hierarchy and exposure exercises previously listed, I also have the patient fill out a checklist of all their avoidance and safety behaviors and put them into an order from easiest to give up to most difficult. We work on the exposures on the website during sessions, whereas the patient will work on the avoidance and safety behaviors on their own, or with a support person. A list of possible avoidance and safety behaviors can be found in Chapter 1.

During the course of treatment with the exposures, you will also want to pay attention to the gradual elimination of safety behaviors. Often patients will be very reluctant to do exposures without using some safety behaviors at first. That may be alright to get someone started, but they need to eliminate all of them once they are tolerating the exposure and certainly by the end of treatment. I let them know this up front and give them a blank three-month calendar so they can pencil in the dates when they will give up each safety or avoidance behavior. I usually suggest they fill in the calendar after they've been working with me for about six sessions. Periodically I check in with how they're doing, but I'm sure to let them know that giving up these safety behaviors is their responsibility and necessary for their successful completion of treatment. Most of our patients do well with this elimination process, but we (and other colleagues who treat emetophobia) do still have dropouts, as this work is very difficult, no matter how slowly and gradually one goes through it.

As your patient progresses, they may become much more astute in catching the more subtle behaviors and you should encourage this when they are ready. Don't jump or press on your patient to eliminate them immediately or they may be reluctant to disclose them. Emetophobia makes people feel out of control and so anything you can do to restore some sense of control, at the outset, is beneficial.

It is amazing the level of creativity that might be at play. Some safety behaviors are quite subtle such as tapping the table or playing with their hair. I used to ask one patient to sit on her hands! Many safety behaviors are thoughts as well which is why it's important to ask the patient what they are thinking from time to time. You will know you are on the right path if, upon stopping one of these behaviors, your patient experiences an initial increase in distress.

Like exposures, giving up safety behaviors can be broken into steps. For example, if a patient seeks reassurance multiple times a day, they can gradually reduce the number of times. If someone chews gum, they can postpone putting it in their mouth or chew it for a shorter period of time. If someone is restricting eating by stopping before feeling full, they can take one more bite.

## The STAR Plan

It's always good to have a plan as patients with emetophobia will run into many challenges between sessions. I tell my patients that up to this point in their lives, their anxiety has been the boss. I will teach them a simple plan (the "STAR" plan) so that they become the boss of their anxiety (see Figure 6.1). This plan can be used outside of session by the patient and taught to a significant other in case the patient needs or requests help with it. In addition, it may serve as a structure for your exposure work in session. I have also taught this plan to children and adolescents with their parents.

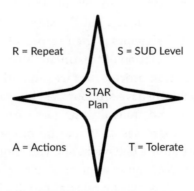

R = Repeat    S = SUD Level

STAR Plan

A = Actions    T = Tolerate

**FIGURE 6.1:** STAR PLAN

## S Is for "SUD Level"

When patients are alone at home, or with a support person, and their anxiety rises, the first thing they should do is to take a SUD reading. This is akin to the ACT understanding of "notice your anxiety." We don't ask patients to notice their anxiety as that can be a ludicrous question if they are panicking. Instead, we suggest they "take note of it," meaning that they note their SUD level. Remember that 0 is no anxiety while 10 is *the worst panic possible*.

## T Is for "Tolerate"

Patients must ask themselves, "can I tolerate or cope with this level of anxiety *without doing anything to change it?*" The latter part of the sentence is key. Patients will be used to using a safety behavior or running away as soon as they feel anxiety. It is important to teach that safety behaviors may be subtle and automatic. I have found that most patients will automatically begin slow, rhythmic breathing as soon as their anxiety rises. This makes sense, since research used to point to it, and the majority of clinicians are still teaching it. It is doubtful that it will have even occurred to the patient to do absolutely nothing when their anxiety rises.

Besides slow breathing, the next invisible safety behavior will be the patient's thoughts. They will have been accustomed to using their thoughts to calm themselves down or control their anxiety. Here are a few examples of a typical emetophobic patient's thoughts:

- You're alright. Just calm down.
- Breathe. Just breathe.
- You're not sick. You're just anxious.
- [That body sensation] is probably nothing. It's just what you ate.
- You felt this way on Tuesday, and nothing happened.

Once a patient starts down the path to using safety behaviors (reaching for gum, sipping water, breathing, thinking calming thoughts) then their phobia continues. It is as if their amygdala thinks: "Good thing they used that safety behavior, or they would have been *really in danger*." Doing nothing "convinces" the amygdala that there must not have been a danger after all because the patient isn't doing anything, and nothing bad happened. As the old joke goes, "Don't just do something. Stand there!"

We have found that most patients can tolerate anxiety levels of 7 out of 10 and below and occasionally some can tolerate an 8. Normally 9 and 10 are too high to tolerate, as most people dissociate at these levels. Pure panic is too much anxiety for the brain to learn anything anyway as it will be completely in survival mode.

### A Is for "Action"

If the patient can tolerate the level of anxiety, then no further action is needed. If the number is too high for the patient to tolerate (9 or 10) then there are *actions* they can take to bring the number down to a level where they can tolerate it. I happen to love using and creating acronyms and I employ them a lot in my practice. If *BRIT* is one too many acronyms, then the patient can simply remember to breathe more slowly and evenly and relax the large muscles in their body from head to toe.

*BRIT* stands for "Breathe. Relax. Imagine. Think." *Breathe* means to breathe as slowly as possible without stopping the breath either at the end of the inhale or the end of the exhale. *Relax* means relaxing the large muscle groups as they have been practicing with the progressive muscle relaxation exercises. Three of these exercises can be found on our YouTube channel (search "Emetophobia Resources" or scan the QR code below), and there are many more available for free online.

*Imagine* means that if the context warrants it, the patient may imagine they are in a peaceful place. Almost every system in our brains except the neocortex (reason, logic) doesn't really know the difference between imagining you are in such a place and actually being there (Jung, Flores, and Hunter 2016; Reddan, Wager, and Schiller 2018). Of course, this action is easier to do on an airplane and more difficult while conducting a meeting.

*Think*—about almost anything—it can take over from the anxious response in the brain. When my grandson was two, he slipped in the bathtub and went under the water for about a second before his mother pulled him up. He then quickly became anxious in the tub: he would cry and shake. As he was quite clever and verbal, I tried this with him, "Can you count with me?" and I began counting "one, two," then pretended I had to think about what came next. As he had to think about it as well at that age, he calmed down almost instantaneously and continued counting, "three, four," etc. I did this only once, he settled into the water, and it was as if the "phobia" completely disappeared. Ah, the neuroplasticity of a two-year-old brain!

**B**reathe
**R**elax
**I**magine
**T**hink

### R Is for "Repeat"

Now the patient should go back to the beginning and start the STAR plan again. What is their SUD level now? Is it tolerable? (Normally, if the person has practiced the BRIT actions like a champion athlete, musician, or dancer, then the level will have dropped below 9, in which case they can try to tolerate it rather than trying to control or lower it.)

## Preparing for Exposure Work
### Take a Baseline SUD Reading

Before beginning exposure, you must take a baseline SUD reading from 0–10. If it is 6 or more, I normally would not start exposure without having the patient take three deep breaths, relax their body, and think of a peaceful place. Exposure will make the patient *more anxious*, so you will need their consent if their baseline anxiety is high to begin exposure and risk taking it higher. Some patients will be very courageous and might say "bring it on." Others may not be ready to start exposure yet. If someone's baseline is 8 out of 10 every time I see them, then it is my opinion they probably need to see a physician for anti-anxiety medication such as an SSRI before beginning exposure. Sometimes they won't agree to that, and you just have to proceed very very slowly. I caution these patients that it will normally take them many more than 16–20 sessions to work through their phobia at this speed.

## Working in Imagination

There is evidence to show that there may be benefit in working with patients in imagination before beginning to work on the exposure therapy hierarchy. Sometimes this is the place where exposure work becomes more of an art than a science. Some patients will find it easier to begin in imagination. However, other patients will be quite triggered by imaginary scenes or scenarios and find it quite difficult. For example, if you have a patient who cannot even say the word "vomit," talk about vomit, or talk about their emetophobia, then they will find it close to impossible to work in imagination. At the other end of the continuum, a patient may tell you quite plainly that they have looked at pictures and videos and nothing bothers them. Don't believe them—"check it out"—by working through the standard hierarchy anyway. A careful reading and noting of the SUD levels of these patients will be imperative.

At first, you will have to use trial and error. In my work with patients with emetophobia I now combine imagination work with the exposure hierarchy *most of the time*. I do this through the questions I ask and by using the "Raise Game" exercise, both of which I will describe below.

### Questions

- Does this change the number from $n$?

When showing a patient a word, picture, or video I first ask, "Does this change the number from $n$ (baseline number)?" Sometimes, for clarity, I add, "Does the number go higher, lower, or stay the same?" I want to ensure that the patient understands their anxiety may go up, but it may also go down. If the patient answers "yes" then you must ask for the new number.

- Can you tolerate this number?

The next question I ask may be the most important, "Can you tolerate that number without doing anything to stop it, lower it, or control it?" If I'm asking the question, they've normally told me a number less than 8, but not always. Some people "get it" right away and are incredibly brave. I have no judgment of patients who are not so courageous. We just approach the exposure more slowly and carefully.

- Where do you feel it in your body?

Question 3 is, "where do you feel it in your body?" Patients need to know that their phobia and rising anxiety are somatic sensations or body memories. Patients answer in several ways which at first was quite surprising to me as I mistakenly thought at one time that everyone experienced a trigger and ensuing anxiety the same way I did. The first thing I felt in my body was a burst of adrenalin like a hand grenade going off, followed by my heart pounding out of my chest. I now describe this feeling to patients as a "jolt of electricity." It is actually a jolt of adrenalin. Now that I have fully recovered from emetophobia, I still get a minor "jolt" from time to time, but I have no trouble tolerating it anymore, annoying as it is. As they go through the exposure exercises, many patients describe a bit of a "jolt" to a higher SUD level and then the number settles down to something tolerable.

Many of my patients describe a feeling in their throat, perhaps a bit like the gag reflex, especially if they look at something particularly disgusting. A significant number of people describe a tightness in their chest, perhaps from holding their breath or their heart rate increasing. Some first notice their palms getting sweaty. Whatever the body sensations are, they are that: body sensations. Notice I did not say "just body sensations" or "merely body sensations" or "only body sensations." These phrases may sound diminutive or dismissive of the experience of someone with a phobia that is ruining their life. Although I understand what researchers mean when they use these terms, I also remember hearing them and thinking, "buddy, you really don't understand."

- What are you thinking?

Another question I sometimes ask if I sense that my patient is not engaging fully with the work of exposure and drifting off into an anxious state is "What are you thinking?" or "What do you think of this picture/video?" If the patient answers with a *feeling* rather than a *thought* or continually answers "I don't know," you will need to point this out to them. It is important while the patient is tolerating the feeling of anxiety that they are able to think. Thinking is a neocortex activity, and just as it was for my grandson in the bathtub, it will help switch the body back over from the sympathetic to the parasympathetic nervous system. It also behooves the patient to experience anxiety symptoms, tolerate them, and get on with what matters to them in life. To do that they must be able to think. This is not to be confused with using distraction as a safety behavior. The difference may lie on that thin line between science and art that is exposure therapy.

## The Raise Game

I play a few "games" with my patients. Sometimes to lighten the mood, I say with a smile, "Let's play a game. It's not a fun game." They're probably better termed "exercises." The Raise Game is an exercise I do when going through easy exposures with patients—things like drawings, cartoons, and pictures of nauseous people. Again, this exercise is more art than science, but I will try to explain it as best I can. Sometimes people seem to be breezing through the exposures. For example, they have a baseline of 2, and none of the drawings or pictures seem to raise their anxiety above 2. This sometimes becomes suspicious to me. I suspect they are telling themselves a story about the image that keeps their anxiety low. For instance, I have a picture of a man on a bed holding his stomach and grimacing. When I ask the patient, "What are you thinking?" they outright tell me something like, "I'm thinking he's not really nauseous; he's just in pain." This is an "aha!" moment for me, as it should be for you when you have a patient whipping through these pictures like they're all of kittens, cars, or wedding dresses. What the patient is doing is a form of *avoidance*. They are avoiding even the belief that the picture is of someone nauseous. So then I ask them to *raise their anxiety*. "Take a moment to look at the picture again, and I want you to raise your anxiety as high as you can. Tell me the number when it's as high as it will go, and then we will remove the picture."

I used to say something like, "when your anxiety is as high as it will go, *or as high as you want it to go*…" But now I leave out the second part because I realized that it won't go higher than the patient wants it to go anyway. This exercise works wonders. Occasionally, someone cannot raise their anxiety, but it goes up several points most of the time. This is because to raise their anxiety, the patient must look at the picture and acknowledge that it is someone nauseous, or someone vomiting, etc. I cannot emphasize the importance of this game enough. So many people I meet online or who come to me for help say that "exposure didn't work for me," so they feel discouraged and hopeless. It didn't work because they weren't really looking at the pictures and videos or were employing invisible safety behaviors. As discussed in Chapter 4, Craske et al. (1991) found that asking subjects to describe what they saw and how they felt about it grounded them in the actual exposure. This technique of "affect labeling" may also be used in addition to or instead of my "Raise Game."

It may seem counterintuitive to have patients raise their anxiety when they've come to see you because it's already too high all the time. But this purposeful raising of the anxiety gives the patient control over it for probably the first time in their life. It's an excellent exercise for "telling" their amygdala, "*I* will decide what's scary, not you."

### That One Picture

As people with emetophobia go through exposure exercises, no matter their background, they will eventually come across that one picture (or video) that really "catches" them. Perhaps they will burst into tears. They may quickly remove the picture and say they cannot look at it. Whatever the reason, there will be a story there. Sometimes people will breeze through all the cartoons, drawings, and pictures of nauseous people and get caught on a picture of someone leaning over a toilet. I have one silly cartoon in the early group of pictures that bothers almost no one, except one woman I worked with who started crying because the man in the cartoon was yelling at a dog, and it reminded her of her abusive father. The rest of the session I spent just listening, empathizing, and validating. By the following week, she could easily look at that picture and continue with the exposure. You never know what may catch a person, so be prepared for it.

### Tears

Not every patient will become tearful or burst into sobs, but it is very common. I always allow the patient some time in silence to really feel their feelings and let themselves cry. They may wish to shut it down, and if so, I encourage them not to. I will then ask them something like, "What was the thought you had right before you became tearful?" They will always be able to tell you. Sometimes I ask a type of psychodynamic question: "Answer this question without thinking about it. How old do you feel?" Not everyone can answer this, but many people will. Whatever age they tell me, it is usually quite young. A follow-up would be, "What happened when you were [that age]?" There was usually something, and that something may never have been validated as something that made them, as a child, feel truly awful. A grandparent sick or dying, a divorce, a move to another city, a beloved pet being put down. Whatever it was, it contributed to their emetophobia in some way, however small. Sometimes it is a self-deprecating thought such as "I'm such a terrible mother" or "I'm such a loser with this stupid phobia." This provides good fodder for therapeutic work with the patient, and one should not rush to shut it down.

I often like to describe our lives as being above and below a trap door, as in Figure 6.2. For many people with emetophobia, they live their entire lives above the trap door. They are married or in relationships, have good jobs, children, and many friends. Under the trap door lies all that happened to them in childhood that contributed to their emetophobia. They will be aware of much of it: some of it they will not. They believe that some vomiting monster lives under the door, and it cannot, under any circumstances, be let out. The entry is bolted down and nailed shut with avoidance and safety behaviors. As long as they can avoid feeling sick or being around sick people, and if they do feel sick, they can reach for ondansetron, ginger ale, or gum, then the nails and bolts remain. If their trap door spring gets triggered, and avoidance and safety behaviors don't work, the door comes flying open, and the Leviathan of panic ensues.

People with emetophobia must learn to unbolt and open the door themselves, albeit slowly and gently. Once *they* open it, they will plainly see that there is no monster under there—just a very sad, scared little child who believed that something yucky but harmless could probably kill them. The adult who opens the door can tell the little child the truth, and they will disappear forever into their grown-up self. This is not a simple "telling." It is a slow, methodical, *learned* telling.

**FIGURE 6.2**

Tears happen when the door flies open and the patient gets a peek at the little child below, either in the arms of that Leviathan monster or all alone and scared. Let them cry for them. Let them be sad for a time. It's a sad, sad thing to have happened to that child. It's okay to cry. But when tears have been dried, it is time for the adult to offer a hand down to the child and help them up out of there.

## ANNA'S STORY—PART 8

Even after deciding that vomiting myself was a big fat nothing, I was still terrified of seeing or hearing someone else vomit. Even if I couldn't catch what they had—I didn't care. I was petrified of them all. But... God kept up God's end of the bargain in curing me of my breast cancer, so five years later, I finally found a therapist who could help me with the emetophobia. To be honest, he didn't help me with the emetophobia. I'd given up looking for someone who understood it or knew how to treat it. But he helped me by listening, caring, and walking with me through it all. I pretty much had figured it out for myself by that time. After all, we had entered the information age. I found other people with emetophobia online. One of them, a woman in the Netherlands, was a computer techy, and around about the turn of the millennium, she uploaded a series of pictures of cartoons and then people vomiting. There was still no YouTube, but I knew every movie that had someone vomiting in it, and I rented them all from Blockbuster. I also ordered a video online from a place called Ambassador Video—some psychologists had made it in Sheffield, England and it showed scenes of real people vomiting.

I got better after about a year. Considering I was making up my treatment as I went along, with about 10 percent of the knowledge I have now, I figured that wasn't bad. The one who screamed and ran up a hill, dissociative and calling for her dead father, volunteered as a hospital chaplain for the final part of my exposure therapy, and eventually stood by the bedside of a vomiting person calmly, and asked if there was anything I could do for her.

## Beginning Exposure and Response Prevention

In our work with people with emetophobia, "response prevention" means preventing oneself (or one's patient) from responding to the exposure with a safety behavior.

### The Word "Vomit"

The first exposure I show all my patients is the word "vomit." They almost universally say it doesn't bother them when they see it. So, I implement a simple test: "Is it a noun or a verb to you?" (Once I embarrassed a patient who couldn't remember which was which, so you can say "a noun—like a thing, or a verb—like an action.") Once you ask this question, they have to think about the word more and picture it. This often changes their SUD level in response because they have been looking at it and trying not to think about it or imagine what it actually is: vomit or vomiting. I may ask them to describe the "picture" or the "movie" playing in their head. Right from the beginning, this has us going back and forth between imagination and what they are seeing on the website or the page.

### Drawings, Cartoons, Pictures of People Before and After Vomiting (four sessions)

It is essential for the clinician to go through all of these levels of exposure with their patients. Some patients will tell you that none of these pictures or even videos bothers them or that they've been through them with another clinician, and it didn't help. Go through them anyway. Then for homework, assign any pictures that may have raised their anxiety even 2 points or more above baseline. I ask them to spend ten minutes per day looking at the pictures until the picture becomes boring to them. I caution them against using any safety behaviors, even their thoughts, while doing the homework. I encourage them to do the homework even (or especially) when they don't feel well, as most people with emetophobia don't feel well a lot of the time.

### Pictures of People Vomiting/Pictures of Vomit (two sessions)

Pictures of people vomiting, or pictures of vomit without any people in the picture, are more challenging to look at because they're disgusting. Make sure you are comfortable with them before the session as the clinician's vomiting in session would be most contraindicated. Nevertheless, these pictures begin in black-and-white or not in focus, so they are much easier to look at than one would think. Keep progressing through the exposures. By these levels, I sometimes have patients look away from the picture after they've looked at it, but I always encourage them to look at it a second or third time if they are finding it difficult. I usually devote sessions 7 and 8 to these pictures.

As you go through pictures of people vomiting, you will find that two things bother all patients with emetophobia, and I am not sure why. First, the volume of the vomit is important in that more vomit means anxiety will rise higher. I have a couple of ideas about why this is: perhaps it relates to how messy the vomiting is, or maybe it means that more vomit would take longer, and perhaps one could choke on it. It would be messy, but there is no mess that cannot be cleaned. Vomiting takes three seconds or less, no matter how much volume there is. No amount of vomit will lead a conscious person to choke.

Second, the consistency of vomit matters to patients. "Chunky" vomit causes them more anxiety than if it is "just milk," for example. This may relate to the messiness factor or the choking factor, but no matter how chunky, messes can be cleaned, and again, no one who is conscious chokes and dies on vomit.

### Check-In with Safety Behaviors (one session)

By session 9, I want to check in with the patient about how they're doing with eliminating safety behaviors. I usually spend the whole session going through the list again with a plethora of responses. I would say that most people haven't given it much thought.

As we go through the list together, I may ask how difficult it would be to give up a particular behavior, as in what are the obstacles, and so on. From here, the patient and I develop a plan for working on the behaviors that are left. I encourage them to look at the next two months on a calendar and "pencil in" which behavior will be given up on what day. I also remind them that once a safety behavior is given up, it is given up for good.

Patients are generally thankful for the respite session from doing exposures and thus are more willing to work together to devise a plan and carry it out on their own. Sometimes we include a significant other in this session, and I coach them on how best to be helpful.

### The Willingness Test

Abramowitz et al. (2019) outline a brilliant little test for people going through exposure therapy. They propose that the clinician ask the patient how willing they are on a 0–100 percent willingness scale to do [insert exposure here]. I use this test when patients are unwilling to do their homework exercise of giving up a safety behavior or approaching something they once avoided (such as a public playhouse with their children). I cannot give you exact numbers, and neither did Abramowitz and his co-authors. If someone says "0 percent willing," they are obviously too afraid to do that exposure, and you may have to break it down into steps. One hundred percent willing is also an easy one, but what about 40 percent? I tend to tell my patients that if they answered 50 percent or more, they are willing to try it at some level. They usually believe me. If the number is in the 30–40 percent range, I ask them, "what will it take for you to be more willing to try this?" It is an honest question because I don't know the answer to it, and I am usually surprised at their ability to figure it out themselves. I follow up with these willingness tests when reviewing the homework at the beginning of each session.

### Videos (four to six sessions)

Most of my patients dread the thought of looking at videos and seem to think that after looking at pictures of people vomiting that the first video they will see will be a thousand times worse. This is part of the catastrophizing typical of anxiety disorders in general.

Some clinicians insist on beginning exposures with videos because they think that will be easy. After all, if someone is afraid of dogs, one might think that a video of a dog would be fairly benign (it wouldn't be). For this reason, I have created a mini-hierarchy of sorts with the videos on our resource page. They start off with a funny commercial of a car that vomits oil it doesn't like, a cartoon of someone seasick where you can't see anything, babies spitting up, and so on. The patient also always has the option of watching the video without sound first, then with low sound, and finally full sound.

Exposure to videos normally takes between four and six sessions, although some patients can be working on them for considerably more.

### Sounds (one session)

Sounds are more difficult than videos for most patients. On our resource page, I give a link to a page with over 100 sounds of vomiting ranging from one second long to over two minutes. There is a description of each sound as well. It is just brilliant. The patient may click on any length of sound or description that they wish, going at their own pace. I spend only one session on sounds and assign for homework at least 20 minutes per day for the patient to work on them alone.

### Expectancy Violation

Expectancy violation refers to the idea introduced by Craske et al. (2014) and reiterated by Abramowitz et al. (2019) that surprising a patient with different levels of exposure, rather than working through a hierarchy from easiest to most difficult, is more effective in the long run. We stated earlier in Chapter 5 that virtually no person with emetophobia would agree to this idea and it may send them running from psychotherapy for good. However, at this stage of work with patients, the clinician will have established trust, and the patient will have more confidence in themselves, so it is possible to introduce the idea now while still having the patient control how it is done.

Simply have the patient, for homework, peruse the internet for pictures of people vomiting and then look for videos of people vomiting. They will probably have to put "throw up," "puke," or some such word into the search engine to find them. I have noticed that my patients, by this time, are quite happy to try this exercise and are very proud of themselves when they accomplish it.

### In Vivo Exposures (one session)

"In vivo" literally means "in life" and refers to exposures that cannot be done with online resources alone. Giving up safety behaviors and particularly avoidance behaviors are each a form of in vivo exposure.

### Smell

Many people with emetophobia speak of the disgusting smell of vomit and assume they could never cope with it. Unfortunately for them, they're not wrong about the smell, and the only way to learn to cope with it is to, well, cope with it. Brian Handwerk (2017) writes of one study done where participants were blindfolded and given parmesan cheese to smell and asked what it was. Cheese-lovers usually identified it as cheese (although not always), and cheese-haters altogether identified it as vomit. Both vomit and parmesan cheese contain high levels of the chemical *butyric acid*. In another study, blindfolded participants were told parmesan cheese was vomit, and vomit was parmesan cheese. They were asked to describe the smell, and those who thought they were smelling vomit, even if they were cheese-lovers, all said it smelled gross or disgusting. The point I'm trying to make is that yes, vomit smells disgusting, but if you thought it was parmesan cheese you were smelling, you might not think so or be nearly as grossed out by it.

Butyric acid is relatively harmless and is available for purchase in the United States by the general public online. You will need the liquid variety for this exposure, which is best done outdoors, as one of my patients asked me how to get the smell out of her house when she tried it inside. Apparently, it can be a bit like a skunk in its enduring qualities. Patients can add a drop or two to a can of vegetable soup or anything else they might find triggering and try getting accustomed to the smell by beginning farther away from it and slowly approaching. If you are meeting with your patient in person this would be a good exposure for you to do together. Again, try it ahead of time so you know you can handle it. Butyric acid comes with a warning that it can burn skin and eyes, so use it cautiously.

### Cleaning Up

Some people with emetophobia are terrified of the mess that vomiting makes or may make in their house, particularly if or when they have children. I worked with one woman whose child had white eyelet linens on their bed, and she was fearful that the child would wake up in the night and vomit on them, and they would be "impossible" to get clean. If your patients express similar worries, there is a two-fold approach to working on this fear. First, talk about the fact that, yes, vomiting is a "situation" (but not a catastrophe), and it would be good to have a plan for cleaning it up. Brainstorm with the patient how they would approach it. Could they first take the bed linens to a laundry sink or outside to hose them down? Then, how would they wash them, and with what sort of detergent or chemical? (You can note that norovirus is killed at 150 degrees Fahrenheit (65 Celsius), which is lower than the hot cycle on most washing machines.) If there is vomit on a carpet or a couch, could they rent a steam cleaner from their local grocery store and purchase a cleaner that works on vomit? (Yes, there is such a thing and it's not at all rare.)

Second, have the patient do a practice clean-up the way the military does disaster training events. They need to mix up some vegetable soup with parmesan cheese and add any food to it they think is vile or will stain (don't use butyric acid for this). Then pour it on those white eyelet bed covers. Once my patient completed this exercise, she became considerably calmer about the whole idea of her child vomiting in bed.

I had another patient once who said he wouldn't know what to do if the baby vomited all over herself in the crib and his wife wasn't home. How would he get her shirt off? Once we talked about this, and I relayed a couple of humorous-but-true incidents of similar proportion involving an explosion of green-apple-two-step and one of my babies, he felt much better about the idea. He then "practiced" by putting old clothes on his daughter and letting her have fun with some chocolate pudding and raspberry coulis. Whatever is on their shirt can indeed get in their hair but trust me, you're headed for the shower anyway.

After checking in with sounds, discussing exposure with smell, and how they feel about cleanup, I introduce the patient to the purposeful exposure exercises they will do on their own. I then usually ask how long they would like to have to complete these exercises before checking in with me again. Some people want two weeks; others want a month to work on them. If the clinician is working with the patient in-office, they may schedule another session and do some of the purposeful exercises together. As I work solely on telehealth, I use this time to see how committed my patients are to working on the exercises alone while at the same time getting them accustomed to seeing me less often.

## Purposeful Exposures

I have entitled this section "purposeful" because it represents a big step for the patient. By this time, they have seen, heard, smelled, and done many things to do with vomit that they never thought they could. The clinician can remind them of this. Now it is time to give up *control*. To do so, we enter some exposures that may make them nauseous on purpose and potentially make them vomit. People with emetophobia have a hard time coping with *uncertainty*, yet it is a part of all life. No matter how small, risk is difficult for people with emetophobia, yet we all risk our very lives all the time by getting into cars. The risk of vomiting when doing these exercises is higher than the normal, day-to-day risk for them. Without using avoidance or a safety behavior, they must *lean into* the fear. Previously, they have always leaned away, sometimes by literally running and sometimes in a more subtle way so as to avoid anything to do with vomiting. *Control, Uncertainty, Risk, Leaning in*. Yes, it spells CURL, but if you hate acronyms as much as David does, you can rearrange the words.

**C**ontrol
**U**ncertainty
**R**isk
**L**eaning in

### Interoceptive Exercises

Much research has been done on interoceptive exercises with anxiety disorders, particularly panic disorder. Clinicians often ask patients to do exercises that would mimic a panic attack such as breathing quickly (to mimic shortness of breath), holding one's breath, running on the spot (to mimic an increased heart rate), etc. Many people we have spoken to with emetophobia describe previous clinicians trying these exercises with them to little avail. They knew that none of these pretend exercises would make them vomit. Unlike panic disorder, with emetophobia, people do not fear panic attacks unrelated to vomiting.

Hunter and Antony (2009) studied the role of interoceptive exercises with emetophobia in a single case study which they reported as successful. Along with the regular exercises described above, they had the subject drink an entire can of soda in one sitting, eat more at mealtimes, practice being dizzy by spinning around in a chair and increase her body temperature by turning up the heat and wearing sweaters. We have added several more exercises thought to be more closely related to addressing emetophobia symptoms. These exercises may be done in any order.

1. Running or exercising: After checking with your doctor to ensure it is safe for you, try running or exercising until you are nauseous. Tell yourself that it's okay if you vomit.
2. Practice vomiting: Mix up some oatmeal, or if you're really brave, some vegetable soup out of the can with parmesan cheese, put some in your mouth, and "practice" vomiting it into the toilet and allow the anxiety to be there without trying to control it.
3. Significant other fake vomiting: If your significant other is a good sport, have them do the practice-vomiting exercise. First, stay outside the bathroom as they make the sounds of vomiting or "vomit" the mixture somewhere other than the toilet. Practice allowing *them* to clean it up without you going back over it later. There are several variations of this one that you can try.
4. Vomit jellybean game: There is an excellent game for sale online called "Beanboozled™." I played it with my family, and it was pretty funny and enjoyable. The game consists of about five colors of jellybeans and a spinning wheel indicating which color a player should eat. Orange ones, for example, may taste like peaches or vomit. Brown could be chocolate or canned dog food. So, you never know if you will get a disgusting one or not and how you will feel if you do. There are also vomit-flavored jellybeans for sale online, which can be ordered and tried as an interoceptive exercise.
5. Gagging: Patients can try to put a popsicle stick, spoon handle, or toothbrush to the back of their throat until they gag. As gagging does not normally cause vomiting, but the other way around, this is an excellent exercise to try. However, it may be the most frightening of all the interoceptive challenges.

### Deepened Extinction

After championing the interoceptive exercises, the patient will probably believe they are finished, but there is more. Craske et al. (2014), when studying a return of fear after exposure therapy, introduced the importance of, among other factors, deepened extinction.

Deepened extinction refers to combining exposure exercises for maximum effect. With emetophobia, there are two primary contexts for these combination exercises:

1. Doing an exposure when the patient already feels nauseous.
2. Doing an exposure when the patient has eaten a large meal.

There are several creative ways to combine exposures. A patient may look at the videos or listen to sounds when feeling nauseous or after a big meal. They may also try any interoceptive exercises when nauseous or after having eaten. Smelling a vomit-like substance or cleaning one up when not feeling well will also be particularly difficult and therefore helpful.

I allow my patients to text me when they are working on deepened extinction exercises because the feeling of being alone, in that no one else really understands how difficult it is, can be quite intense and sometimes overwhelming. This practice is not for every clinician and isn't absolutely necessary.

### Living with Risk and Uncertainty

Unfortunately, the uncertainty of "living life" with abandon and joy, or as they say in ACT, "living your values," is too much for many people with emetophobia to handle. They are afraid to travel, go to school, go out socially, and generally enjoy life. Again, part of the recovery process with emetophobia involves living with uncertainty. Will today be the day the patient throws up? Maybe. Maybe not. Nobody knows. For some reason, we find that children will more readily accept this change in perspective than adults.

Sometimes I tell my patients that on the west coast of Canada, where I live, runs the Cascade fault line. There is a risk of a major earthquake at any time, probably in the next 50 years. The school behind my home, where my grandchildren attend, has regular earthquake drills. When the alarm sounds, the students are supposed to get under their desks so that they are not injured by falling debris. At home, one should get under a table in an earthquake. I point out to the patient that we in Vancouver cannot live our lives underneath a table, and in fact, people do not. They go out shopping, go to theaters and concerts, go to work, etc. People with emetophobia must learn (slowly and gradually) to get out from under the table and begin living their lives, even though there may be a (minuscule) risk of vomiting.

### Leaning In

After finishing the exposure work, patients need to go out into the world, "leaning in" to the fear. Leaning in means living with the uncertainty that vomiting could happen at any time. It means taking that risk and carrying on as if you do not have a phobia. If you want to be "normal" (meaning neurotypical, as in not having emetophobia), then you must behave as though you are normal, like everyone else. Would your non-emetophobic partner or neighbor sanitize the whole house with a much-too-strong bleach solution just because someone in the house drank too much and vomited once? Do your classmates avoid tables weeks after someone seated there was sick? They would not, so leaning into the fear means that you shouldn't either.

## Cognitive Work

As discussed in Chapter 3, emetophobia is closely related to OCD, so many people with emetophobia often have obsessive thoughts. People with emetophobia may be higher or lower on the Emet-OCD continuum (Figure 2.1 in Chapter 2). For those high on the continuum, this cognitive work may not be helpful as obsessive thoughts will keep returning again and again. If this is the case, the patient should try to do nothing and just let the thought be there. One can simply take note of it and leave it alone.

Those low on the Emet-OCD continuum may try to challenge their thoughts. Two questions are asked to "test" the thought:

1. Is it true?
2. Is it helpful?

I have found that generally with emetophobia, the anxious thought is indeed true. For example, they may think, "I could get food poisoning from that chicken," which is true, even though it is not probable. However, the thought about the chicken does not pass the "Is it helpful?" test because thinking that thought, let alone dwelling on it, will not help anyone overcome their emetophobia.

In cognitive therapy, it is often suggested that people challenge thoughts by asking if the thought is *probable* or that people try to think about the probability of the anxious thought happening. Vomiting is never probable, not even with taking chemotherapy. However, many with emetophobia don't care about probability because they have such a difficult time accepting any possibility or living with any risk whatsoever. I had one patient who had not left his house in eight years. He once told me, "Even if there is only a 0.0000000000001 percent possibility that I might vomit, I'm not going to go out."

### Theory A vs. Theory B

A non-threatening understanding of emetophobia to present to patients is the "theory A vs. theory B" model developed by Salkovskis (1996). With emetophobia, *theory A* is that vomiting is 100 percent awful and cannot be tolerated. You are at risk of vomiting at all times. If you do vomit, you will lose all control, perhaps embarrass yourself, and the vomiting may never stop. You cannot cope with not knowing when you may vomit. Therefore, you must avoid vomiting at all costs by using safety behaviors and avoiding anything that might lead to vomiting, even in the rarest of circumstances. (We have found that this "theory A" is extremely common with almost all people with emetophobia.) *Theory B* is that *worrying* about vomiting is the real problem. All the avoidance and safety behaviors don't likely prevent vomiting anyway. Avoidance behaviors ruin your life and prevent you from confirming that vomiting is not probable, or not that bad. No one likes vomiting, but it isn't harmful, and you could certainly handle it if it happened.

It is best to ask the patient which theory they now adhere to and what that means for their life. If they lived according to theory B what would their life look like? I have talked with my patients about these theories and find that for some, looking at their life this way is a real eye-opener. Others seem to know that theory B is true, but they don't know how to stop living as if theory A is true, even though they want to.

## Automatic Negative Thoughts (ANTs)

People with emetophobia, much like all patients with depression or anxiety, usually have several ANTs. I like to give my patients a list of typical ones for emetophobia and ask if they look familiar:

### Common ANTs with Emetophobia

1. Catastrophizing: Vomiting is terrible, horrific, my worst nightmare, etc.
2. Magical (superstitious) thinking: If I say it or talk about it, I will jinx myself, and I'll vomit; I got sick 20 years ago on Thanksgiving, so now I'm afraid every Thanksgiving; I was wearing a particular shirt when I vomited so now I'll never wear it again or it will make me vomit.
3. "Why me?" thoughts: Why am I like this? Why do I panic? Why am I so stupid? Why does vomiting exist in the world?
4. Bargaining with God or praying to God not to vomit.
5. "What if" thoughts: What if I vomit? What if it's not cooked? What if I get carsick? What if I catch norovirus?

There are a number of ideas about how to rid oneself of ANTs, such as:

- Imagining the thought being written on paper, then crumpling it up and throwing it away.
- Imagining the thought being put in a box on a shelf for later.
- Imagining the thought being written on a leaf that falls into a nearby river and observing it floating down the river.
- Saying to oneself, "that's not a helpful thought."
- Saying to oneself, "I don't need to think of that right now."

Note that if the patient is high on the Emet-OCD continuum, none of these exercises will work and should not be attempted. Sometimes patients will tell you that they get into "arguments" in their head by trying to counter an ANT, but the ANT argues back. This is indicative of the patient having obsessive thoughts, which should just be left alone. These mind arguments cannot be won.

## Self-Comfort/Self-Soothing

Self-comforting thoughts may have, at one time, been encouraged when treating anxiety but we know from research that they are ultimately safety behaviors and not helpful in the long run. In our clinical experience we have found that most of our patients have gone to great lengths to convince themselves that they aren't sick, or they won't vomit. And yet their phobia remains. Instead of these thoughts, we encourage our low Emet-OCD patients to respond to the thought with, "No comment," the silent treatment, or something like "Maybe I will [vomit]; maybe I won't. I'm not answering." High Emet-OCD patients should just allow the thought to be there and do nothing about it. Here are some examples of self-comforting thoughts which serve as safety behaviors and so are ultimately not helpful, and if possible should be given up:

- You're okay. You won't be sick.
- You felt like this last Tuesday, and you were fine.
- You never vomit. You always feel this way and you're never sick.
- It's just gas/bloating/hunger/feeling full, etc.
- You never touched your face so you can't catch anything.
- Your mom never had morning sickness so you're okay.
- Mom/spouse just reassured me so I'm fine.
- Spouse never caught it, so I won't either.
- This picture/video isn't real.
- I'm in control. I can stop myself from vomiting.

There is a difference between these self-soothing thoughts which function as safety behaviors and positive cognitions which do not. The test is whether the thought assumes vomiting is dangerous and should be avoided. So, for example, "you're okay; just breathe" assumes that if you're not "okay" and you vomit then you're in a dangerous situation. Positive cognitions such as "vomiting isn't dangerous or harmful" are acceptable.

## Positive Cognitions

- Vomiting is not dangerous or harmful.
- Vomiting can't hurt me, so I don't need to be afraid of it.

- It doesn't matter if I vomit.
- Even if I vomit, I will be okay/safe/fine.
- I am not in any danger.
- This feels dangerous but it isn't.
- If someone vomits it's not a catastrophe; it's just a situation.
- Vomiting is normal, natural, and neutral.
- I am safe enough.

When I volunteered as a hospital chaplain for the last part of my exposures, I had the positive cognition "I am not in any danger" written on a little card that I carried in my pocket. Before I would go into a patient's room, I would take a deep breath and read the card to myself. Once I was in a family meeting and a patient felt nauseous and asked for a basin. I put my hand in my pocket just to feel the card and it was enough to help me remain in the situation despite my anxiety, which rose to about 8 or 9 at that time.

Positive cognitions are not to be used to control or lower one's anxiety. Rather, they are more like a "pep talk" to give oneself before entering an anxiety-provoking situation. They may also be used to help the patient stay in a frightening situation despite rising anxiety or, if possible, even panic. Ensure that if they choose something like "I am not in any danger" that they don't mean "I am not in danger of vomiting" as opposed to "I am not in danger *even if* I vomit."

### Future-Focused Thoughts

Generally speaking, thoughts that focus on any future situation are anxious thoughts. I encourage my patients to identify these thoughts which are always some variation of "what if I vomit?" Leaving these future-focused thoughts alone, taking note of them and doing nothing is really the best thing. Allowing them to circle around and around may lead to a panic attack. If a patient's anxiety is spiraling up, a good exercise for them to try is to focus on the here and now. I teach them to change the words "what if" in their minds to "right now." By that, I do *not* mean for them to say something like "right now I'm not sick." Instead, encourage patients to use as many of their five senses as possible to ground themselves in the present day and time.

- Right now I can *see* the cherry tree out the window.

- Right now I can *hear* the children playing outside.
- Right now I can *smell* dinner cooking in the oven.
- Right now I can *feel* my feet on the floor.

I used to ground myself in the present by saying the current date and time, and that I was *x* years old as in "It is 2023 and I am 49 years old" (okay, 65). Sometimes this grounding with date and age works well because the patient, when anxious, is actually experiencing a somatic flashback to when they were a child. Even if a vomiting incident happened before they can remember it, *their body remembers it*.

## Reassurance

Reassurance-seeking is a safety behavior and as such needs to be stopped. If significant others are giving reassurance, they need to be coached not to give it either. Usually encouraging significant others to answer questions honestly, with "I don't know" is enough to get the person with emetophobia to stop asking. Some of the ways people with emetophobia will seek reassurance include:

- Will I vomit from this?
- Do you think this is cooked properly?
- Are these leftovers still okay?
- Will I be okay if I _____?
- Do you think I'll throw up today?
- Will exercise make me sick?
- Should I throw out this yogurt?
- Do you think this restaurant is safe?
- Will I get motion sick on the plane/train/bus?

Clinicians often are asked for reassurance or at least we're asked questions that seem like reassurance. People with emetophobia can come around to the back door and sneak reassurance into the house as well. I am careful not to answer any questions such as the ones above, or any that seem to be similar. However, I do reassure my patients all the time by giving them simple facts and honest answers. I will only answer these questions *once*, however, otherwise they get the response "asked and answered!" Some of the reassurance questions and answers that I do give are noted in the following table.

| Question | Answer |
|---|---|
| Do you think I will get morning sickness from pregnancy? | I can tell you that of the thousands of women with emetophobia that I have heard and seen online, very few get morning sickness. There are also excellent and safe drugs on the market which prevent morning sickness. |
| Will taking an SSRI make me sick? | I have never heard of a person with emetophobia being sick as a side effect of an SSRI. |
| Do you think I'll throw up on the plane? | I've never heard of a person with emetophobia throwing up on a plane. |
| Will I vomit from anxiety? | If you've never vomited from anxiety before, you won't now. |
| Can I catch norovirus from kissing my husband who just had it? | No. Norovirus isn't transmitted through kissing. |
| Can I catch norovirus from being next to my child who has it and just vomited? | Yes, that is entirely possible. |
| Can I eat food after the "best before" date without getting food poisoning? | Usually, yes. It depends on what it is, and on how long ago the best before date was. |
| Will I get motion sick from the car ride? | Not if you haven't before. Adults who get motion sick also got motion sick as children. |
| What if I vomit after waking up from surgery? | Anesthesiologists have special drugs they give in a cocktail during surgery, so you don't vomit when you wake up (see Chapter 8). |
| What if I vomit while I'm under anesthetic? | That never happens. |

## The Sticky Note

When I first meet my patients, I ask them when the last time was that they vomited. I ask them what it was like, or what they thought about it after it was over. Almost without exception they answer something like "It wasn't that bad." However they word their answer, I write it word-for-word on a sticky note and put it inside their file (Figure 6.3). Later, when the ERP work gets to be pretty intense, I remind them of what they said about the last time they vomited. I encourage them to also write these words on a sticky note and keep it nearby. Some folks take a picture of the sticky note and use it as the wallpaper on their phone. Sometimes it is the best thought to remember at just the right moment.

**FIGURE 6.3**

## Telehealth

I have been working with people with emetophobia on telehealth for 12 years. I began as soon as I discovered Skype in 2010. The first thing I thought when I discovered it was that I could offer to work with people with emetophobia all over the world. My licensing body, like many of them at the time, had no rules yet about telehealth or working with people outside of the province where I am licensed. I am so thankful for this because it allowed me to work with people with emetophobia from many countries and cultures.

Once Covid-19 hit, almost all clinicians started using telehealth. Some have continued, and many have offered to continue if patients wish to do so. I stopped using Skype as it wasn't thought to be PIPA/PIPEDA (equivalent to the USA's HIPAA) compliant. Luckily, there are now many excellent telehealth programs for clinicians to use. I can now only practice psychotherapy in my own province, but I do offer a 16–20 session educational program online for emetophobia provided participants have their mental health looked after by someone else.

Nevertheless, in our clinical experience with over 300 patients, most over telehealth, the medium works well for people with emetophobia. Stubbings et al. (2013) found in a controlled trial that CBT in-person or over telehealth worked equally well for anxiety and depression treatments. Berryhill et al. (2018) in a systematic review of videoconferencing and anxiety treatments also found no difference between the virtual and face-to-face groups. Song and Foster (2022) agreed, although they emphasized the need for clinician training to optimize the experience.

Telehealth is convenient for patients as well, especially if they are afraid to leave their homes. Normally I have the patient open an internet window on their computer so they have control over opening the pictures and starting the videos. If people are meeting with me on a device other than a computer, I can share my screen with them to show them pictures and videos. Patients have also "brought me along" to in vivo exposures via their smart phones. I've been with patients virtually in their bathrooms to "practice" vomiting as well as to classrooms and movie theaters.

I believe that one day licensing bodies will see the value of telehealth and of psychotherapists specializing in disorders as I did and allow us to see patients outside of our licensed geographic area with specialized training, and under certain rules and conditions.

## What Not To Do

1. Ask, tell, encourage, or suggest that the patient should vomit.
   We've discussed this a few times already. If you inform your patient of the opposite, in fact, you will win a great deal of their trust. Reassure them that they don't need to vomit to overcome the phobia.
2. Start too far up the hierarchy.
   The proper hierarchy is this: words about vomit, sentences and paragraphs, drawings and cartoons, pictures of vomit, pictures of people before and after they vomit, pictures of people vomiting, videos, sounds, interoceptive exercises, in vivo work (perhaps going somewhere such as a hospital ER to see if they might see someone vomiting), deepened extinction. *If you start anywhere on this hierarchy but the beginning you risk frightening your patient away.* They might tell you "I can look at pictures and videos because they're not real." Don't believe them. Start at the beginning anyway.

We've had more than one patient tell us that their last clinician suggested upon intake that they should go sit in an ER and wait for someone to vomit. They've also had clinicians tell them to go home and look on YouTube for videos about "vomit, puke, throwing up." Most of those clients never went back to therapy. If they did go back they often got shamed by the clinician for not doing the homework. Some were told to come back when they were ready to face their fears. Others were told that they were non-compliant with treatment; some were asked to discuss what benefit or payoff they got from having a phobia, and why did they want so badly to keep it. Which leads to point 3.

3. Blame the patient.

If your patient isn't getting better, ask *yourself* what you may be doing wrong. Very few patients are actually lazy, non-compliant, treatment-resistant or unwilling to face their fears. They're just more scared than you previously realized and what you're asking of them may be too difficult.

4. Ask the patient to do weird things.

We have seen, heard, and read many stories of clinicians who are treating OCD-contamination asking their clients to do things like touching toilet rims and such. We do not suggest asking them to do anything more than what a person without emetophobia would be willing to do. Some say the pendulum has to swing way the other direction to come back to center. Even if this is true, it's doubtful you could convince a person with emetophobia to do something extreme as the anxiety is so severe. Besides, isn't our goal to have our patients become more like people without emetophobia? I once watched a TV show on extreme OCD, a residential program, where the participants were asked to go into an alley and open up a dumpster. Then they were supposed to wipe their hand on the inside of the dumpster and lick their hand. The clinician did it first. But not before he had looked inside and declared that it looked like someone threw up in there. Most of the clients were hysterical, crying, and screaming. I figure they must have signed one heck of a contract not to just say "Oh *hell* no" and walk out. Perhaps it was all scripted. But here's a true story: one of my podcast guests (Christie 2020b) went to a therapist who listened to her "story" for all of about ten minutes and then said "What if you licked your shoe? If you lick your shoe I'll lick mine," she declared, ever so bravely. The patient said she wouldn't lick her shoe for ten million followers on Instagram. Then the therapist walked over to her computer keyboard and licked it. The patient started to think that she had signed up with a crazy person for a therapist. She couldn't wait to get out of there. The sad thing is that after leaving she felt ashamed, guilty, and hopeless. She went on to describe this experience to other people with eme-tophobia as "exposure therapy" in such comments as "I tried exposure therapy (or "I tried CBT") once and it was horrible and didn't work for me." When a client comes to us making this declaration, by the way, we must first ask them to describe the exposure therapy or CBT in detail.

Don't ask your patients with emetophobia to do weird things that no ordinary person would do.

## ANNA'S STORY—PART 9

My grandson threw up in the car (and not even in a garbage can but all over himself) a few years ago when we had been driving for about an hour. Unlike on the way back from Disneyland I didn't panic. It gave me a rush for a second but that's about it. I like to think of it now as more of the rush of an extreme sport. I calmly drove to a gas station and went inside to buy paper towels and wet wipes while my daughter tended to the little boy. Then I got back in the car and drove the remaining 15 minutes to our destination.

## Chapter 7

# TREATING CHILDREN WITH EMETOPHOBIA

## Dr David Russ

The vast majority of patients I have treated with emetophobia have been children. Typically, treatment is sought by parents in crisis because the symptoms are dramatically disrupting school, eating, sleep, and/or daily activities. Despite the disruption, it often takes quite a bit of investigation for parents to figure out exactly what is scaring their child, mainly because it is common for children to avoid certain words or talking in any way about vomiting lest it evoke anxiety or nausea.

Emetophobia has been mentioned with enough frequency in the last few years that it has become easier to identify. However, don't be surprised if the parents present the problem as non-specific anxiety or something else.

### Family Affair

Emetophobia is a family experience. As a clinician, it is essential to understand that a family has been "hijacked" by this phobia. Although the child has the phobia, the impact on the family can be quite dramatic. It is incredibly confusing when someone (adult or child) is experiencing the onset of an anxiety disorder. For example, it is common for people who experience their first panic attack to think it might be a heart attack. Often, by the time someone realizes it is an anxiety disorder, the cycle that perpetuates it has been established. This is true of emetophobia.

Because the anxiety symptoms are quite intense, families may respond with similar intensity. Symptoms may be met with frustration and attempts to convince their child they should not be afraid. Usually, this degrades into discouraging arguments. Alternately, reassuring their child or removing their child from the situation triggering the anxiety is normal. They don't realize that in most cases, both arguing and compassionate rescuing and reassuring end up reinforcing the cycle.

At first, a caregiver doesn't know that avoiding and reassuring must be repeated continually to prevent a "meltdown." For example, if one's child is nauseated and doesn't want to go to school, it is normal to keep the child home. This is especially true since the Covid-19 pandemic. The relief a child feels is so striking that it is incredibly reinforcing. The urge to avoid school will dramatically increase as well as the level of anxiety if required. Other demands to prevent anxiety will grow. If a child is anxious at bedtime, staying and comforting them until they fall asleep is pretty normal. Soon it becomes a "necessity," or no one sleeps for hours. It becomes commonplace for a caregiver to hear repeated variations of, "Do you think I will get sick today?"

Certain foods become safe or unsafe. The food served becomes limited, and mealtimes can become very complex and frustrating. The anxious child may have a separate menu or eating arrangements from the rest of the family. To keep the peace, families stop using words that could trigger anxiety and make all kinds of changes to prevent triggers. Adults can't go on dates without repeated texts or tearful calls. Sometimes they just give up.

Trying to keep a child calm is both altruistic and self-interested. Caregivers may alternate between compassion and "tough love." At first, no one realizes that trying to keep the peace *when an anxiety disorder is involved* completely backfires. The family will present for treatment as confused and discouraged because nothing seems to be working. Part of the treatment consists of persuading caregivers to eliminate all these accommodations gradually. They will need a plan as much as your patient.

Children have limited power over things, so they may resort to extreme behaviors to convey their distress. Adults can often choose to avoid almost anything. If kids are required to do something anxiety-provoking, attempting to escape can evoke extreme emotion and behavior. It is not uncommon for a caregiver to report that their child is saying something like, "I don't want to be here!" or "I should just die!" Of course, anyone would be horrified to hear this. It is very rare for a child (ages 6–11) to be clinically depressed (Ghandour et al. 2019), so this is likely an expression of the greatest form of protest a child can imagine. If a child throws a tantrum, it may not be an issue of bad character. Nor does it warrant a diagnosis of oppositional defiant disorder or the like. Rather, it is one of the limited ways a child can express the amount of fear being experienced.

Caregivers will often express concern or feel guilty that they might have done something that caused the anxiety. As a clinician, you will likely have opinions on the impact of parenting on the development of anxiety disorders. I have been a therapist for a long time. I have supervised and trained dozens of clinicians. There is the pervasive idea that all problem roads lead back to parents. I am not going to discuss that idea at all. I mention it to say that the caregivers in your room are very distressed, and this is almost certainly not the time, overtly or covertly, to bring that into the room.

Generally, I take the position with adults that their worry that they caused this, or that they have failed, is a relatively useless exercise with anxiety disorders. There is no way to even answer that question. Successful treatment of the phobia tends to dissipate the guilt, and I prefer to get on with that rather than spending time on parenting problems. Of course, if an adult is clearly handling this poorly, it will need to be addressed. You can decide if these caregivers need treatment, either from you or via a referral for individual or couples therapy.

## Caregiver Intake

My first session is with the caregivers. If possible, I prefer to have all the significant caregivers present for this session. I consider it preferable but not obligatory. Signed consent from all legal guardians is required whether they are present for the session or not. This appointment is vital for gathering background, determining specific triggers, understanding the impact on the family, and possibly most importantly, understanding and agreeing to the treatment. I spend part of that initial intake explaining the nature of the therapy. To summarize, "We are going to make your child anxious on purpose." There must be both understanding and consent to the process in principle.

Once treatment of the child starts, I like to have *one* adult involved in the ongoing treatment. By involved, I mean present during the sessions with the child. I have found that during telehealth appointments, the adult may leave the meeting because of other demands, so it is essential to be clear with this. I am not quite as insistent about this with older teens (ages 15–18).

There are several reasons I think it is crucial to include an adult in the treatment process for emetophobia:

1. Follow-through. Getting a child, or anyone for that matter, to do something terrifying is just short of miraculous. To do exposures, one must disobey their nervous system. Your secret weapon is a motivated caregiver who is very invested in their child getting over this phobia. In my experience, children are more likely to have a successful outcome because an adult provides the structure and encouragement to do the homework. A motivated adult wants to sleep, go out to eat, or go on a date. Tap that motivation, and you will help everyone. Additionally, during treatment, you will be training that adult to take your place. One reason I love working with kids is that they are used to doing what other people want them to do. That is part of why I have more success with children than adults.

2. Elimination of accommodations. As mentioned, a family with good intentions will accommodate the child to keep the peace and provide comfort. Once the anxiety becomes apparent, most caregivers scramble to reduce their child's intense anxiety. There is something horrifying when your child is in absolute panic, and you feel relatively helpless to do anything about it. They will reassure their child ten times to avoid a 45-minute meltdown. They need not only to understand the ERP process but see it in practice. They need to see that their child can handle the anxiety and share that experience with their child. When it is time, there will be a gradual and systematic reduction of all the accommodations and safety-creating behaviors. I introduce that from the beginning but will not start requesting changes

in safety behaviors done at home until at least 3 or 4 steps into the hierarchy. My working principle is that if I run into a hard "no" regarding eliminating a safety behavior (or exposure), I don't push (this may be a behavioral "no" rather than a verbal one). Instead, adjust the step until you get a willingness to do it. Also, it will be you, the clinician, who will be prescribing these changes. That will go a long way toward limiting the arguments and power struggles since the adult can say, "This is what the doctor said to do, not me."

3. Safety. Almost always, the adult that is most involved and who feels most safe to the child is the one who will come to treatment or be present if meeting via video. Having this adult present creates a sense of safety for the child, which is very important, especially at the beginning. I have had young patients claw their parents, run into traffic, run from the room, or climb under furniture because of the fear. Happily, the most extreme behavior has not happened in my office, but likely only because of the safe adult. (Running out of the room is more common if the session is via video.) The child will also watch if their caregiver feels safe with and trusts you. This will help the child to trust you.

4. Observation. I want the caregiver to see what happens when their child is anxious and to model a calm, non-judgmental response. This helps to stabilize what is happening. It is severe anxiety, not rebellion. Everyone in the house is probably scared or frustrated to some extent. It can be so helpful for a caregiver to see a different way to interact with their child regarding the phobia.

5. Collaboration. The adult gets to participate in their child's healing, rather than just the clinician. We are a very temporary part of a patient's life. That the patient experiences mom, dad, or caregiver as an essential part of healing is life-changing. If only the patient is seen, there is the possibility of poor communication or pitting the clinician against the parents. Adult, child, and clinician all working together minimizes this in an already charged system.

6. Mediation. Obviously, the adult knows their child far better than you, and the child will need the caregiver to mediate by

communicating if you misstep. When you are working with emeto-phobia, it is like walking through a crowded market. One misstep, and you spill a stack of oranges. Sometimes children, especially younger patients, are too polite to say no to you but will tell mom or dad they are scared. I consider myself a good observer, but I have ended sessions thinking everyone was just fine, only to be told by the adult that the child completely fell apart afterward.

7.  Training. I want the adult to understand what to do with excessive anxiety. Medical practice has framed our assumptions about so many things. Caregivers need to replace the assumption of an expert prescribing medication with a process of learning and action. Understanding and observing their child's hard work will hopefully replace the frustration with encouragement and appreciation. Kids need an adult to go through this process with them. One cannot drop off their child with the clinician and get them back fixed. Not with this. This is training, not fixing.

I appreciate the idea of having all the primary caregivers involved in the ongoing sessions. That being said, it turns into couples therapy far too often. If adults or caregivers are not on the same page on how to handle this in the household, it is better to have sessions without the child present. As mentioned, I have found that one consistent caregiver being involved works best. Sometimes logistically, that isn't possible, and you will need to be prepared for a different dynamic with a different adult, especially as children get older. For example, one caregiver may be blunter or have missed prior sessions. Or a child may be more argumentative with one caregiver than another.

It may be essential to address with the caregivers managing one's temper. Only a saint would not get frustrated and upset over the impact of this phobia. However, most caregivers will confirm this: expressing anger or frustration simply escalates things. No matter how maddening, encourage your patient's caregivers to try to remain neutral. At least on the outside. It is quite common when a child is upset for caregivers to become more verbal and more insistent in their attempts to manage their child. When a child is highly anxious, it will have the opposite effect. The reasoning part of their brain may be completely overwhelmed and even shut down. It is better to use fewer words and wait to discuss it once everyone is calmer. "Trying to reason with someone before they are regulated won't work and indeed will only increase frustration (dysregulation) for both of you" (Perry and Winfrey 2021, Chapter 5, Figure 10). This is not always possible depending on the situation, but it is a worthy aspiration.

In families with two caregivers, often one adult is the "softy," and one is the "toughy." Encourage them to try to stop fighting about that. Both are doing some things wrong and right. You may have limited time with both, but this is worth discussing with them. Let them both know, as the therapy proceeds, that you will do your best to help them adjust their interactions toward a common goal of helping their child. The softy must realize that to get better, the child has to feel anxious and not get rescued. The toughy must be patient and eliminate anything that might be shaming or guilt-provoking. Their child's alarm system is doing what it is supposed to do but at the wrong time. There isn't something defective in their child.

## Initial Treatment Session(s)
### Ground Rules and Safety
After the initial greeting and connecting at the first session with the child, there will be a point when you switch to talking about the reason we are meeting. I frame it this way:

> Talking about anxiety can cause anxiety. I want to ask you a favor. Will you let me know if you are getting too anxious if I don't notice? This is important to me. I know you are probably really polite and are not supposed to say "no" to adults, but you have my permission to do this. If you still are not comfortable, you can give mom (or the caregiver present) the "look" or signal that you are anxious. If you get nervous, we can change the subject until you feel calmer, okay?

I tell kids they are the expert on their anxiety, and they have to teach me about it.

As Anna pointed out, while working with adults, you may introduce the word vomit early in the treatment. However, both of us tell children that we will not use any words about the thing that scares them until they say it is okay. When I ask them about their fear, I listen carefully to what words they use. I listen for what I think is the safest of those words and, even then, ask permission before using them. For example, I might say, "You used certain words to describe *the thing*. Can I use those words, or would you prefer we just call it *the thing*?" Even with permission, I still use them sparingly. Establish a safe environment with clear expectations. I once heard a story of someone going to a psychiatrist and the psychiatrist used the word vomit repeatedly after being told it was anxiety-provoking. That child and the parents were so upset, they refused to go back. Patients will interpret that as the clinician not having a clue about the phobia. Often the adult and child are familiar with the word emetophobia. I don't recall anyone reacting anxiously to the use of that word and it is likely safe to use early on.

While gathering background, if I pick up any caution from the child at all, I ask them if they would prefer for mom (or caregiver present) to tell me about it, and then they can add or correct it as needed. Except for timid kids, they will soon jump in. Expect the information to be pretty sparse. This is up to you and your therapeutic approach, but I gather relatively little additional background during the first session. Good intake forms with information about siblings, educational level, household members, medical background, prior treatment, etc., are important in gathering the essentials.

Anna, rightly so, spends more time on this with adults. Developmentally, children are at the beginning stages of managing difficult emotions. Knowing what to expect and how treatment works are more important in early sessions since children and their caregivers are quite anxious. Additional history will unfold as treatment proceeds. I have already acquired some of that information in the caregivers' prior appointment(s). For many kids, the origins of the phobia may be experiences of either being sick or seeing others get sick. However, there may not be a clear beginning. It isn't essential when treating children to know the origins of the phobia. Also, keep in mind that talking about memories is likely anxiety-provoking, and until exposures are scheduled, I prefer limiting triggers if possible.

I ask my patients about specific symptoms that will invariably be present, for example asking for reassurance, restricted eating, scanning for sick people, etc. I use the occasion to say, "Do you know how I know about that? It is because I see so many people with this." This is the occasion to normalize (not minimize) the phobia, process, and prevalence.

## Softening the Hard News

It is important to reframe the whole process. No one wants to do exposures. What we are aiming for is a *willingness* to do them. It is all about finding motivation and removing imagined obstacles. Children, with the consent of the adult(s), have less choice when it comes to being in treatment. Giving children a clear explanation and some measure of choice or control is essential to help offset the fact that they are, to some extent, likely being compelled to come.

I tell kids they can't make regular anxiety go away. It is part of life. What we are after is the "extra" or unnecessary anxiety. It can go away, but there is a process. Wishful thinking that there is a miracle cure or some way to make the world safe must be discredited. To do that, a clinician needs to connect ERP to everyday processes. ERP is hard, there is no point in trying to disguise that from your patient, but there must be a clearly understood purpose. An analogy is an excellent way of doing this.

An analogy doesn't have to be as debilitating as emetophobia to work. If you know your patient loves sports, that is where you find your analogy. If your patient likes to dance, you go there. For example, you can ask your patient about the first time they rode a bike without training wheels. Break the process down into steps. Each step is likely to have a challenge that is at least a bit anxiety-provoking. (I like using the word "challenge" to describe exposures.) For example, going down a big hill, riding a bigger bike, or riding farther from home are all examples of challenging steps. Learning to swim, being tested academically, performing in front of others, or going to summer camp are also possibilities. Different examples will be needed for teenagers. Even if your patient doesn't have the experience you are looking for, they will almost certainly know others who have or can easily imagine it. Critical points in the analogy are that the experience will cause at least some anxiety and that as you repeat the challenge, it becomes more comfortable.

After repeating and learning the skills to handle it, the alarm goes down. You are both normalizing and generalizing the universal process of mastering something. There isn't a shortcut to this. ERP is best framed as learning and mastering something new, not fixing something broken.

This is a good place to describe how the brain works (covered in some detail in Chapter 5). You will need to develop a way to make the information developmentally appropriate. Keep in mind the limited attention span of children. Anna describes the limbic system as the reptilian brain. That may need to be translated differently for children. I often describe it as the three-year-old brain. It is really good at noticing when something is wrong or scary and will throw an absolute tantrum. However, it doesn't bother with things like how things work and what is real. It wants what it wants. The other parts of the brain need to be back in control. Who would make big decisions based on what a three-year-old thinks?

## Process, Not Event

In addition to the idea of mastery and learning, is conveying the process of habituation. With repetition, you get used to something. I like to use this example, although it isn't strictly the same because it involves pleasure and not anxiety. I will say to my patient, "Imagine a song you love. Now imagine listening to it 100 times in a row." Eventually, it doesn't evoke the same enjoyment. There are any number of possible analogies. What you are looking for is something that, when repeated, gets boring. I explain that this is why you have to do something over and over. However, make sure it is clear that your patient will initially feel the distress they want to escape. If the expectation is quick relief after an exposure trial, your patient may feel like they are failing or think it isn't working. The initial goal is to handle the distress and repeat it enough. That will lead to the ultimate goal of significant anxiety reduction or elimination and rapid, resilient recovery if there is a trigger. Imagine playing baseball, and you catch a fastball. You notice it hurts, and then you move on to throw the ball and continue to play.

Another aspect of the process to be introduced is separating what you need to master into steps. I often use the treatment for allergies as an example. (First, check to make sure your patient is not afraid of shots. I try to leave out the word "shot" regardless.)

When you go to the doctor, they put just a bit of what you are allergic to in your body. You must wait for 20 minutes or so to make sure they don't give you too much. Too little and getting used to the allergen would take forever; too much and your body over-reacts. Over time, the doctor gradually increases the amount of the allergen, but it doesn't cause a stronger reaction because you are used to what came before. That is what we are going to practice here.

I go out of my way to make this point to my child patients: I would rather start with too little than too much. Then we can increase until we find the right balance. This is, again, an excellent place to reinforce the need for feedback if something is too much. The few times I have heard of ERP going wrong, the clinician introduced too much challenge too soon.

I then convey the idea that there are two parts or sides to this.

1. Part one is that your patient will face the scary thing in small doses. We start with low challenge and work our way up. I say to my patients, "The amazing thing is that if you master each level of the challenge, the next challenge won't be much stronger. Just like the allergy treatment." I remind my patient that they are feeling worried anyway, so we will just schedule it with the "dose" they are willing to handle. "Better than being surprised, right?" Getting good at something often hurts. I will use the analogy of someone learning to run long distances. To run long distances, you keep running even when it hurts. Anxiety is like that. You must handle the anxiety when you do the challenges until it gets easier and easier; it is part of mastering it.

2. Part two is practicing responding differently. Instead of trying to escape, we will practice dealing with it. Instead of trying to make a feeling go away, you can give it "permission" to be present. It is there anyway. If this is really challenging, we can practice for a few minutes only. Stopping safety behaviors, like trying to escape the negative feeling, is as important as facing the fear. I say to my patient, think of it this way: Why would you do something to be safe unless there was a possible danger? A safety behavior assumes danger, threat, or intense distress. So each time you do something "safe," you reinforce the belief that something is dangerous.

## The Hierarchy

We have covered the standard hierarchy in Chapter 6. With children, there are some modifications in the vignettes, images, and videos, so they are age-appropriate and relevant. For example, an adult vignette might be about a party where there is drinking. A child vignette might be a party at a fun restaurant. Please keep in mind that any hierarchy template may need some modification. For example, we have written several exposure paragraphs for anxiety around bedtime. A sample is on our website[1] at the end of the paragraphs section (scan the QR code below). The main paragraphs are designed to be as universal as possible, but if there is a particularly triggering situation or experience, a clinician should create a vignette for that. An option for exposure practice is having your patient record the paragraph and play it at home.

As Anna stated, at the beginning of the hierarchy, we intentionally try to avoid surprises. I always ask permission before administering an exposure. At least until well into the process. I also describe what is coming in a general way. I try to avoid anything higher up the hierarchy but include things already covered. For example, if we are on step one, words, I won't put the word in a sentence. By the way, caregivers will often do that, and you will need to discourage it gently. If we are practicing the word "barf," a caregiver might say something like, "Remember in the car when your brother said he would barf?" Your patient will probably handle that okay, but you are setting the terms for the treatment, so your patient needs to know there are no surprises. Of course, life has surprises, but that can be addressed further along the process.

On the other hand, as you proceed you should combine exposures for deepened extinction. For example, if you are on the step looking at illustrations of people vomiting, you could use trigger words when

---

1    www.emetophobia.net/exposure-for-kids/paragraphs-for-kids

you are describing what your patient is about to see: "The next cartoon is of a dog *puking*, and there is a *lot of it.*" Only include *prior exposures* that have been *successfully completed*. I would encourage you to err on the side of caution until it is clear how your patient will respond.

Prepare to adjust. Clinically it works much better to increase an exposure that is too easy than back off one that was too hard. Even if your patient seems fine, you may not know until the caregiver tells you their child freaked out in the car after the session. *Go slowly!* You are unlikely to get the same feedback you get with adult patients.

A crucial principle to keep in mind while doing exposures is this: if something is too hard, don't force it. However, don't *abandon* it. Find a way to continue in that same direction but make it less challenging. For example, if the exposure is of a video your patient will not view, adjust it in a way they are willing to view. See the notes on how to do that below. What you don't want to do is give up viewing that image. I have often had children refuse to do an exposure, and we go back to something previous and continue practicing. Inevitably, once they have a chance to think about it, they are willing to continue forward, although it might be the next session. I encourage patients over and over, if you are doing anything in the direction of facing your fear, no matter how small, it is a win. This principle is important for your patient and caregivers to understand when they are doing homework. Make sure there is *no* guilt if something is too hard. I tell patients that knowing it was too hard is just good information we all need to help us do this well. But there is no giving up. There are several ways to adjust an exposure, and some of the ways we have found helpful are below. These are designed to reduce the anxiety or raise it if the exposure is too easy, as Anna described in Chapter 6.

1. Say it quietly or loudly or vary the tone. Saying a word softly or turning off the volume on a video will usually make something easier. I almost never introduce a video exposure with sound. Then low volume, then normal volume. I don't have the option of making it very loud, or the clinicians in the offices next to me would be pounding on the wall, but it might be something to consider if that is possible. You might say a word with a deep voice or higher pitch.

2. Break it into parts. Very anxious children may not be able to

tolerate even words. Typically, I start with either "sick" or "get sick." (If you are pretty good with dad humor, you can start with something ridiculous like "smelly feet.") Use the caregiver's input and observe your patient carefully for how alarmed they might be. If my patient looks very reactive, I will immediately hide the word depending on whether I am using a device, paper, or whiteboard. Then I will write something like "s_c_" instead of the complete spelling of sick. If I start with that, I let everyone try to guess. I use a Keynote or PowerPoint presentation quite often. The first slide is all the letters scrambled. The next slide, once it is guessed, is the actual challenge. Another example is breaking images into parts by covering up a piece of it, or if introducing a paragraph exposure, doing one sentence at a time.

3. Increase distance and/or decrease size. The farther away a trigger is, the less distress it causes. I have moved to the corner of my office, so the image I am using is less distressing. Making the exposure small will also be effective if you are working on a telehealth platform. If a patient has to squint to see something, that almost always causes them to move closer, which is a tacit exposure itself.

4. Blur the image. This may require a bit of technical expertise on your part, but you can blur an image to make introducing the exposure doable.

5. Change the speed. When I am using video as an exposure, depending on the level of distress, it is less challenging to stop the movie and treat it like a still shot. You can also, depending on the application, speed it up. Faster is usually easier. This makes sense if you think about it. When imagining throwing up, people with emetophobia believe there is far more chyme (partly digested food) and that it lasts much longer than it does in reality. So, slowing down a video will be more challenging because it is more like the fear. Speed is generally also a factor when practicing verbal exposures. It will not be uncommon if your patient "speeds" through a sentence, for example. Slowing that down will increase the challenge.

6. Use black and white, grayscale, and color. This obviously applies to visual content. Generally, the challenge follows in the order just listed.

7. Change how the exposure is introduced. For example, I will ask my patient, "Do you want to see the word first, hear me say it (or spell it), or have your mom (or caregiver present) say it?" That gives your patient a bit of control but also gives you information about the trigger. Once you have that, check back on it periodically because it might change or become irrelevant, but use that pattern going forward. A solid operating principle is that anxious people prefer if someone else does it first. Be prepared for exceptions to the rule.

8. Focus. When looking at images or videos, I will draw attention to irrelevant details such as shoes, ages, background, etc. This purpose is to draw attention to the image and continue pulling your patient into it. It also can shift attention for brief moments, reducing the anxiety for just a moment without having to completely refocus attention.

9. Use humor. Being funny is on a continuum. If you are comfortable using humor, this can help when introducing exposures. Kids with emetophobia take it very seriously (of course). For example, you can say "barf" as if a dog was barking. You can use a high pitch or silly accent. However, if you pick up that it is not working, it's best to stop as it might come across poorly. You can still lighten up the process using games, funny comics, or pictures. If there is a funny video you think your patient will like, take a couple of minutes when things are tense and laugh.

We know that if something causes at least some anxiety, gets repeated, and safety behaviors are eliminated, then the anxiety will go down. What is unknown is how long this might take. I wish I had known more about this when I first tried ERP with patients. Your first exposures as a clinician can be pretty scary. You won't know what to expect in several different ways. (Did I mention going slow at first?) Once you start, your patient and caregiver must be prepared to continue. When I first started using exposures, I remember thinking, "Please work, please work, please work." Your patient needs to continue the exposure until the anxiety begins to subside or their tolerance is clearly getting stronger. Do not be shocked if it goes up a bit at first. Ideally, the distress needs to come down from the peak before you stop the exposure (based on their SUD score). It doesn't have to be gone completely, just lower during any given trial.

Generally, to result in a noticeable impact, we have found that exposures for this phobia take 15–30 minutes if they are moderately challenging. That is just a range. You won't know until you have experience with your patient. Since most sessions are an hour, maybe less with younger children, don't start a new exposure toward the end of a session until you know your patient quite well.

We have carefully thought through exposures designed for children, and they are available on our website[2] (scan the QR code below).

Prepare your patient that their anxiety might be, in general, higher than usual once they start this. They may be fine now but get anxious about the exposure later. The thinking will be something like, "I may be fine now, but what if I freak out later when I am alone or what if this makes me nauseated later?" Address this and suggest, if they are willing, they can continue to practice by not fighting the feeling and do the exposure again. I like to say something that implies a certain specialness. "Only the toughest kids can do that." Never underestimate a subtle appeal to ego. Remind them they are changing how they respond to the anxiety, so it makes sense that it will be a bit stirred up. One of my favorite analogies is from Dawn Huebner's (2007) book, *What to Do When Your Brain Gets Stuck*. Imagine a kid and mom checking out of a store. The kid wants candy. Apparently, it is a matter of "life and death." Mom says, "No," and the kid throws a tantrum. Mom gives in. Next time at the store, the same. After a few times, the mom is determined to say no. She does that, and the tantrum is titanic. Then next time not so much and after repeating several times, no more tantrums. I then apply this to my young patient, "You have

---

2   www.emetophobia.net/exposure-for-kids

to put up with some tantrums from the three-year-old part of your brain at first, but if you say 'No' consistently, the tantrums will stop."

If the anxiety has not dropped by end of a session, normalize it. That is relatively rare if you are going slowly, but it can happen. Hopefully, you have prepared them that anxiety is necessary for exposures. What they feel is nothing new. Moving *toward* a trigger is new, but not the feelings. If a patient expects some anxiety, they are less likely to be surprised. Ask them what they have done in the past and give them permission to use it, even though it will likely be eliminated eventually. Remind them that it will pass. If you stay calm, the caregiver and child will benefit from that.

If the anxiety is much higher than anyone expected, remove the trigger, switch topics, and return to earlier exposures. If they are either panicking or close to it, they are usually crying. Compassionately wait for them to calm down. Don't rush that; it may take several minutes. Own the mistake and express that you will be even more careful going forward and adjust the step. Acknowledge that this is hard and thank them for the courage they have to come and do this. Remind them of previous times this has happened and that they will feel better after a time. If you have not done so already, consider using the rest of the session and possibly the next explaining and practicing the BRIT exercises Anna described in Chapter 6.

While going through the steps, check-in frequently on SUD scores. That will help you adjust to the challenge of the exposure. If you get low scores, you can speed up going through the steps or use the raise-up technique. If high scores, you can take more time on each step or adjust the intensity. I say at the beginning of treatment that I will ask a lot about this so my patient will know what to expect, and explain it helps to adjust the treatment to work best for them.

Sometimes a numerical score doesn't fit a young patient. I don't push that; I just switch to a verbal option with low, medium, and high. You can create more variables with low-medium or medium-low, with the first word having the most weight. With younger patients (ages 6 or 7), you can draw a vertical line, and they can mark from low to high. Some kids get overly precise and can take a long time to figure out the number. I might switch to something else if that happens. If this suggests some perfectionism, it might be worth addressing, but usually I prefer to bypass it until later.

On occasion, your young patient may be on the autism spectrum. I have only worked with patients that were high functioning. Essentially the treatment will be the same, although it may take quite a bit longer, and you may have to repeat each exposure trial many more times than usual to have the desired effect. Additionally, you may need to significantly increase the variability (not of the steps) of the exposures if your patient has trouble generalizing. If you have limited experience with neurodivergent patients, you may want to collaborate with a specialist or refer to someone experienced with treating anxiety disorders with that population.

## Homework

A counseling session is usually around an hour. Practice sessions at home will be much shorter. I am generally pleased if they are done at all. I am thrilled if they are done repeatedly. I usually caution, especially at the start, that they only practice what we have done during the session. If the patient and caregiver are motivated, they can move ahead once they are confident in the process. This assumes the existing exposures are significantly less anxiety-provoking. Cutting out the safety behaviors will almost always have to take place at home if they are behavioral. Mental safety behaviors you can work on in session.

The same process Anna described regarding safety behaviors can be used with children. Once they understand safety behaviors, most older children (ages ten and older) will begin to catch when they are doing them. If you ask about them, or they tell you about them, expect them to be a bit "coy" about it. The trouble is that they know you are going to ask them to stop these behaviors, and they may not be ready to do that. I typically encourage it but also give them a sense of control about when and how much they give up. You can break up safety behaviors into steps, just like exposures. For example, if they are restricting food so they won't feel full, a first step might be to eat one more bite, even if it is quite small.

Where and when an exposure is done for homework can vary the reaction. For an exposure, you can suggest they start with the safest place or time at home and work toward more difficult challenges. As you can imagine, saying "puke" at the kitchen table would probably be more challenging than other times or places. School is often the most triggering situation, so eventually you will want them to do exposures on the way to school.

I am frequently surprised to discover a new safety behavior with a patient. It is hard to discover them because patients don't think of them as problems. They think it is just normal coping. I was working with a young woman, and we went through the whole hierarchy successfully. She was back at school and doing great. There were just a couple of things left to tackle. Then she mentioned, almost as an afterthought, that she was scrubbing her desk, chair, pens, and pencils every morning with hand sanitizer. Check on this frequently and refer to the list in Chapter 1. However, keep in mind that patients can be pretty clever in creating and hiding safety behaviors.

When I first began to practice as a psychologist, I only worked with adults. In the process of focusing my practice on anxiety disorders, I started to see children. It is an absolute delight. Virtually every child patient who goes through the process we have described is substantially, if not completely, better. The dropout rate is less because the family is invested as well. While some of the research has suggested emetophobia might have a chronic course, that is absolutely not the case if you can help a child using the treatment process we have described. We know there is very little research to back up that claim, and we are providing anecdotal evidence that is likely full of our bias. Nevertheless, if this book trains more clinicians and possibly stimulates more research, that will change, and we know it will benefit those with this debilitating disorder.

## Chapter 8

# OTHER TREATMENTS AND MODALITIES

A variety of different treatment approaches have been used with emetophobia including hypnosis (McKenzie 1994; Ritow 1979), a single session of flooding (Wijesinghe 1974), transactional analysis (Kerr 2013), combined cognitive, dynamic, and family therapy (Manassis and Kalman 1990) and group therapy (Ahlen et al. 2015; Philips 1985). Although we are not aware of any studies using neurofeedback to treat emetophobia, we are aware of some anecdotal evidence it might be helpful. There are a few published studies using it to treat OCD and a recent meta-analysis suggests there is preliminary evidence that it may be efficacious (Zafarmand, Farahmand, and Otared 2022). Given the similarity of OCD and SPOV, such research hints at the possible benefit.

## Clinical Behavior Analysis

Clinical behavior analysis is associated with traditional cognitive behavioral therapies but focuses on the context and function of the problem behaviors. It borrows heavily from ACT and mindfulness as well. The single case presentation by Mitamura (2019) describes a 22-year-old Japanese female. Although terrified of vomiting she had never vomited previously. She wore a mask, avoided crowded places, and washed excessively. She was given a battery of pre-assessments. Treatment included exposure with a focus on a mindful approach. The therapist employed a values-based approach as well to help the patient challenge the belief that she would not be approved as a legitimate member of the community without a full-time job. The exposures were helpful in reducing her anxiety but not her sense of well-being. The value approach was effective for that. Assessment scores were also positive although the author notes treatment was impacted due to time limitations.

## Eye Movement Desensitization and Reprocessing (EMDR)

EMDR was developed by Francine Shapiro in 1988 to treat soldiers with PTSD. The patient is asked to recall a stressful or frightening situation, focusing on the negative thoughts, images, and body sensations while the clinician moves their fingers left and right so that the patient's eyes track from side to side. The idea is that the anxiety felt is a result of unprocessed emotion, and the bilateral movements (which can also be sounds or tapping) help to process the information.

de Jongh, ten Broeke, and Renssen (1999) studied EMDR and the treatment of specific phobias. EMDR was found to be "more effective than placebo control condition, but less effective than exposure *in vivo*." Several phobias were treated successfully with EMDR, however the researchers raised the question as to whether more complex phobias such as choking, vomiting, or driving can be treated successfully with it.

In a case report by de Jongh and ten Broeke (1994), a woman was relieved of her vomiting phobia using EMDR after a single session and the fear had not returned at a four-month follow-up.

de Jongh (2012) describes a case of a 46-year-old female with emetophobia. Her diagnosis was determined through a standardized diagnostic interview, and she was given the SCL-90-K, Dutch version. Treatment consisted of four sessions of EMDR. The first three involved the recall, reprocessing, and desensitization of early traumatic memories. The fourth session was to install a future template which is a blueprint for positive action in the future. Her score on the SCL-90-K dropped from her pre-score of 275 to 121 (average). At a three-year follow-up she reported some mild distress, but she was still very happy about the outcome.

I (Anna) underwent several EMDR sessions with the therapist who ultimately helped me overcome my emetophobia. I found the process fascinating, and I learned a lot about the origin of my phobia.

However, it didn't make a dent in the anxiety I felt around it. I'm glad that I had the EMDR and have since sought to process some other troubling events in my life through EMDR with the same therapist. Yet, in all the thousands of people with emetophobia that I've talked with online and the hundreds that David and I have treated, we have yet to find any for whom EMDR did away with their phobia entirely as described by de Jongh in these published cases. There also has been no further research replicating these studies.

## Dialectical Behavior Therapy (DBT)

Since many people with emetophobia—particularly when it is severe—are sometimes misdiagnosed with borderline personality disorder (BPD), these patients are often offered DBT to treat their emetophobia. In our opinion, just as BPD is a misdiagnosis, DBT is an ineffective treatment for emetophobia.

DBT is a derivative of CBT and emerged in the 1980s because of failed attempts in the 1970s to use CBT with chronically suicidal patients and other complex, difficult-to-treat, and high-risk conditions such as BPD, non-suicidal self-injury (NSSI), and/or parasuicide behaviors (suicidal behavior without death as a goal), and later with substance abuse disorders (Linehan 1987).

With suicidal patients, and those having difficulty with emotion regulation, CBT focused on change. This was experienced by patients with difficult or complex disorders as being invalidating of their experience. Many patients simply shut down, stormed out of the room, or verbally attacked the clinician. Focusing, on the other hand, on validation and acceptance also didn't work. Patients assumed the clinician simply didn't understand them and wasn't helping.

DBT is a multi-modal approach to therapy. The patient receives individual therapy, group therapy, and is afterward able to consult with the clinician by phone. The clinician also consults with other clinicians regarding the specific case. In individual DBT therapy, the patient is encouraged to set goals and define them. They are taught skills in both individual and group therapy for distress tolerance, mindfulness, and emotion regulation. DBT theory is based in part on dialectics, social behavioral theory, and Zen practice.

Since people with BPD lack emotion regulation skills and distress tolerance it is easy to see how someone with emetophobia could be misdiagnosed with it. When people with emetophobia are distressed and terrified, and they are in the presence of a clinician who does not appear to understand them, they can easily become hysterical or angry, so it appears as if they simply need to learn better distress tolerance. They actually need much more than that, and a different approach altogether.

Some patients with emetophobia also do have a bona fide BPD diagnosis or are also addicted to substances. In these cases, DBT is absolutely called for; however, once a course of DBT is completed the patient will still need treatment for their emetophobia with ERP.

## Metacognitive Therapy (MCT)

Metacognitive therapy is related to cognitive therapy but instead of focusing on the content of thoughts, the cognitive processes themselves are the targets of treatment. Metacognitive beliefs such as "worry will help me prevent something bad from happening" or "I cannot control my worry" are examples.

Simons and Vloet (2018) described treatment of three female adolescents with emetophobia using MCT. Examples of the procedure included encouraging the patients to view thoughts about throwing up as unimportant. "Every day you worry you could vomit. Do you think this thought is an important message to you or just a thought?" (p. 62). They also encouraged experiencing a thought in a non-reactive fashion and then letting it go. All scores on post-tests dropped from clinically relevant to normal. The treatment was relatively short (8–11 sessions) and none of the three subjects dropped out prematurely.

We certainly see that this approach could be relevant to many cases of emetophobia, but there were several limitations to this study, and we think it is unlikely to work as a stand-alone approach to treating emetophobia.

## Transdiagnostic Treatment

Dargis and Burk (2018) presented a single case study using transdiagnostic treatment with a young woman with emetophobia. Transdiagnostic treatment looks for similar characteristics across all disorders in similar categories. For example, in all fear-based disorders it is suggested that "defensive reactivity" is a common underlying feature (Lang, McTeague, and Bradley 2016). The authors report using this approach without any *explicit* vomit-specific stimuli.

Sessions 1–10 were spent primarily on psychoeducation about anxiety disorders, treatment planning, and behavioral activation. They presented a cognitive model of anxiety and addressed time management, as academic performance was an additional stated concern to emetophobia. Behavioral activation encouraged her to seek enjoyable activities that were rare because most activities caused anxiety.

Sessions 11–22 were exposure exercises including interoceptive exposures like spinning in circles. She created an exposure hierarchy and was encouraged to complete an activity on it at least three times per week. Since she expressed some social anxiety, she completed exposures related to that as well.

Sessions 23–30 included completing in vivo exercises from her hierarchy as well as learning to challenge distorted beliefs around throwing up as well as other areas of excessive anxiety. Sessions 31–46 focused on applying the previous strategies so the anxiety no longer disrupted her life.

Certainly, there are characteristics that underlie all anxiety disorders and there is clinical utility in learning a treatment protocol that would apply to any kind of anxiety. However, it appears to us that most of the treatment was exposure for emetophobia. Although claiming there were no explicit vomit cues, sessions 11–22 were full of implicit vomit cues that function much the same. Her hierarchy consisted mainly of eliminating safety behaviors. We are not sure how interoceptive exposures would not be considered explicit as it is just a different sensory modality from, for example, visual triggers. We applaud the treatment of the comorbid disorders but do not think they have demonstrated that explicit exposure is unnecessary.

## Competence Imagery

Moran and O'Brien (2005) present a case of an 11-year-old female with emetophobia who is unresponsive to systematic desensitization. Apparently imaginal, video, and in vivo vomit stimuli did not elicit significant anxiety other than avoidance and discomfort. The competence imagery treatment consisted of pairing anxiety-provoking stimuli like scenes of people vomiting with her imagining areas in which she was competent, like playing musical instruments or swimming laps. The treatment lasted for 16 weeks and her Y-BOCS score dropped from 14 to 3.

While interesting, her previous treatment was not clearly described other than it was not effective. She was repeatedly exposed to triggering stimuli including imaginal, video, and in vivo. It is difficult for us to determine if the exposure or competence imagery actually made the difference. We suspect the patient was employing safety behaviors in her prior treatment while doing exposures resulting in less reactivity. It is unknown if the prior exposure material and that of the researchers were different. We think the competence imagery may, in fact, be a safety behavior or alternatively be replacing her prior safety behavior, but that 16 weeks of exposures likely resulted in the habituation of her anxiety.

## One-Session Treatments

A recent development in the treatment of specific phobias has been one session treatments (OST). Typically, the session will last for several hours using graded exposure, psychoeducation, and modeling by the provider. OST has been used with effect for phobias with spiders, animals, injections, claustrophobia, dentistry, and flying (Keyes et al. 2020).

An adaptation from OSTs is time-intensive treatments. These are longer sessions over a shorter number of weeks. They have been adapted for other anxiety disorders such as OCD, PTSD, and PD. Keyes et al. (2020) conducted a "proof-of-concept" study to determine if time-intensive treatment would be effective with SPOV. The results were comparable to a study with a more conventional randomized controlled trial using CBT by Riddle-Walker et al. (2016). Participants found the intensive days fatiguing and hard to do. Advantages included a lot of material covered in a short time, less homework, more tasks covered and confidence to do exposures because they built on work just completed.

Although there is evidence that time-intensive treatment could be very effective with emetophobia, the research is based more on injection and animal phobias. It is our opinion that OST would be contraindicated for emetophobia, which has more in common with illness anxiety and OCD. Complexity makes time-intensive treatment quite clinically impractical. Persuading reluctant patients to participate in an intensive treatment and trying to schedule the treatment are just two of the possible complications.

## Medications

Many people with emetophobia are reluctant to take medication of any kind because they believe the side-effects will make them vomit or they "don't believe" in medications. However, there are times when medication may be indicated, and there are medications that patients are already taking that are contraindicated. It is therefore important that non-prescribing clinicians familiarize themselves with these various medications so that they are aware of what is going on medically with their patients, or what might help them if prescribed. We recommend that every clinician purchase a copy of Preston et al.'s (2021) *Handbook of Clinical Psychopharmacology for Therapists* or similar. If you're fascinated by the world of pharmaceuticals as they pertain to mental illness, it's an excellent resource. If not, it is still a good reference in general and the "Quick Psychiatric Reference to Medication®" inside the back cover is worth the price by itself. Clinicians such as us who cannot prescribe medication should not discuss medication in any way that would be considered medical practice. However, it behooves us all to know and understand what medications are being prescribed to one's own patients as well as the dosage and the manner of titration. If anything seems out of sorts, we can at least recommend that our patient get a second opinion or see a psychiatrist about their medication if they do not have one already.

I (Anna) once had a patient who "didn't believe" in taking medication, although he hadn't left his house for eight years because he was afraid he might vomit in public. No matter how small we broke down the exposure of going outside, he was still terrified the whole time and unfortunately excessively relieved when he returned home, which only reinforced the phobia. After working with him for over a year, I finally convinced him to try medication and he was prescribed 100 mg of sertraline. Within a few months, he had a job, was going out with friends on the weekend, and enjoyed shopping and walking his dog.

Many parents are reluctant to put their children on medication, and this is understandable. We both have children, and we understand that medication is a difficult decision for parents. This seems to be especially true for all mental illnesses including anxiety, depression, ADHD, and various conditions for children on the autism spectrum. The main factor to consider is this: is your child *suffering*? There is no reason for kids to suffer needlessly when there is medication that might help them. Of course, the decision should not be undertaken lightly, and we don't recommend it lightly either.

### Anti-Emetics

As we have stated, we are neither physicians nor pharmacists. Our knowledge of pharmaceuticals such as anti-emetics comes from years of hearing about them from patients, looking them up and reading about them in various sources including Preston et al. (2021) and Canadian Pharmacists Association (2021), speaking to our own physicians and pharmacists about them, and general knowledge. We do not recommend any medications with our patients; however, some readers will be psychiatrists or other clinicians who are able to prescribe or recommend. We include this discussion as well so that non-prescribing clinicians can help patients determine if something they are taking is being used as a safety behavior or the medication seems to be problematic (e.g., has side effects), in which case one would refer the patient to their prescribing physician.

There are several good anti-emetics available by prescription as well as over the counter. Generally, their use is a safety behavior for people with emetophobia and so gradually weaning off, if they've been taken regularly, is indicated. As effective as most of these medications are, many people with emetophobia do not find them helpful for nausea. This is because their nausea is caused by anxiety, so the only medications that may help them are those with a tranquilizing effect.

Some anti-emetics can be useful from time to time and in various contexts with emetophobia, as we have outlined in the following table.

## Prescription

| | |
|---|---|
| Ondansetron (Zofran) | May help patients with emetophobia understand, when it doesn't work for their nausea, that the nausea is anxiety-based only. Many patients believe ondansetron to be a miracle drug as it is used for chemotherapy-induced vomiting, however any benefit is likely a placebo effect. As a safety behavior, its use should be discontinued. |
| Metoclopramide (Reglan, Metozolv ODT) | Speeds up stomach emptying for patients with comorbid gastroparesis, although it should not be taken long term. |
| Prochlorperazine (Stemetil, Compazine) | This medication is one of the antipsychotics which can be used to treat non-psychotic anxiety as well as nausea/vomiting. Its main use is for motion sickness and nausea associated with migraines. |
| Domperidone (Motilium) | May also be used to speed up stomach emptying for patients with comorbid gastroparesis. It can be taken longer term than metoclopramide. |
| Droperidole (Inapsine) | Much like the more-well-known haldol, droperidole will quickly calm an agitated patient as well as control nausea and vomiting. Used in hospital emergency or psychiatric situations. |

## Over the Counter

| | |
|---|---|
| Dimenhydrinate (Dramamine, Gravol, Cinnarizine) | Typical use is with children and adults for motion sickness. Used in many hospitals post-surgery. Has some tranquilizing effect. Comes in suppositories for children when they can't keep anything down during gastroenteritis. Should not be used routinely (as a safety behavior). |
| Promethazine (Phenergan, Histantil, Sominex) | An antihistamine commonly used for motion sickness and anxiety before surgery. Prescription only in Canada: over the counter in some other countries. The likely benefit experienced by emetophobics is a placebo effect as it has a sedating quality. As such it is a safety behavior and should be discontinued. |

*cont.*

| **Over the Counter** | |
|---|---|
| Pepto Bismol | As the ad jingle goes "nausea, heartburn, indigestion, upset stomach, diarrhea." Thanks to this ad, Pepto is often used as a safety behavior. Extended use can cause constipation and other side effects. Any of the aforementioned symptoms could be tolerated as practice in ERP. |
| Various anti-gas, antacids, and simethicone | All used as safety behaviors. Only indicated by physician's instructions for comorbid GERD. |

## Post-Operative Nausea and Vomiting (PONV)

Gan et al. (2014) published consensus guidelines for anesthesiologists stating that combination pharmacologic therapy is more effective than any single anti-emetic for post-operative use. Some of the combinations that can be used are as follows:

1. Droperidol and dexamethasone.
2. 5-HT3 receptor antagonist and dexamethasone.
3. 5-HT3 receptor antagonist and droperidol.
4. 5-HT3 receptor antagonist and dexamethasone and droperidol.

Laypeople will probably not have heard of many of these PONV medications as they are used in and after surgery and are not prescribed for other uses to the public. We include this section for the purposes of giving solid facts to people with emetophobia who need surgery. Although we normally would not reassure a patient with emetophobia, their need for surgery may be a medical necessity in which case presenting them with the fact that there are a plethora of drugs that can be given to them in surgery to prevent vomiting may be in order.

## Morning Sickness

Many women with emetophobia fear pregnancy because of the countless stories that are shared over the internet and on social media. In particular, there is an extreme but rare form of morning sickness known as hyperemesis gravidarum or HG of which women with emetophobia are understandably very afraid. With HG, women may vomit all day every day. They can lose alarming amounts of weight or end up dehydrated and hospitalized.

Thankfully, there is an excellent medication on the market specifically for morning sickness known as Diclegis in the USA or Diclectin in Canada (Nuangchamnong and Niebyl 2014). It has recently been approved in the UK and many other European countries under the brand name Xonvea. It is a delayed-release combination of doxylamine (an antihistamine) and pyridoxine (vitamin B6). According to Madjunkova, Maltepe, and Koren (2014, p. 208) "the fetal safety of no other drug has been as extensively studied as the delayed-release combination of doxylamine and pyridoxine." This drug has been on the market in Canada in various forms since 1957 although it was briefly taken off for further testing but went back on in 1979. Most pregnant women with morning sickness describe this medication as a wonder drug.

As many people with emetophobia are fearful of taking any medication at all, and particularly in pregnancy, it may behoove the clinician to reassure the patient that Diclegis has been approved as an FDA Category A—the category indicating the safest to use in pregnancy (Nuangchamnong and Niebyl 2014). We include this information here because in speaking with people with emetophobia online it seems as if not all doctors are familiar with this drug or its safety. Women considering pregnancy should specifically ask their doctor or OBGYN about it. I (Anna) have had patients whose doctors "refused" to give it to them. These patients need to find another doctor who takes into consideration the suffering of all women, not just women with emetophobia, in pregnancy. There is no reason why women with emetophobia cannot have children, as many thousands have already, and their mental health during pregnancy should be treated with as much care and attention as their physical well-being.

### Anti-Depressant Medications

As we discussed in Chapter 6 under "Preparing for Exposure Work" if a patient has a baseline SUD level of 6 out of 10 or above then it is very difficult to do exposure work. If a patient describes their average SUD level over the past month as 8 out of 10 or higher then we are really faced with a problem. It is in one of these two circumstances that we usually discuss medication with a patient.

## SSRIs, SSNIs, Atypical Anti-Depressants

Many prescribing physicians are unwilling to give people with emetophobia anti-anxiety medication because they say it "doesn't work for specific phobias" (Benjamin et al. 2000). We submit that perhaps the reason it doesn't normally work is that a specific phobia is triggered by the stimulus and when there isn't one then the patient isn't anxious. Think for a moment about someone with a clown phobia. The patient may only be triggered by clowns on television or clowns at a parade. If they don't turn the television on or don't go to the parade, then they're perfectly at ease and don't need medication. However, emetophobia isn't like that. If someone is only afraid of seeing others vomit and they live alone then perhaps it is similar. But most people with emetophobia are terrified all the time as they fear their own bodies. Anti-anxiety medication has been, in our clinical experience, a life-saver to a great number of patients. According to psychiatrist, researcher, and emetophobia expert David Veale: "SSRIs have some benefit in OCD when prescribed in the maximum tolerated dose for at least 3 months" (personal communication, July 2, 2022).

SSRI stands for "selective serotonin reuptake inhibitor." SSRIs have been around as anti-depressants since about 1987. SNRIs (serotonin norepinephrine reuptake inhibitors) are newer, introduced about a decade later. A variety of even newer anti-depressants have been dubbed "atypical." According to the Mayo Clinic (2019) the Food and Drug Administration (FDA) approved these atypical anti-depressants to treat depression. A number of them have also been used to treat anxiety.

In our experience both with our own patients and talking with people with emetophobia online, the type of anti-anxiety medication prescribed depends on the symptoms of the patient, their medical history and other medications used, and the personal preference of the prescribing physician. I (Anna) have had many patients be prescribed the drug mirtazapine with good success as it also has anti-emetic benefits and increases appetite. However, I've had several patients whose doctors refuse to prescribe it for them, stating that it's only for depression. I also had a patient who had a bad allergic reaction to it and five years later still has not recovered, although this is extremely rare.

### Addiction

As opposed to the views of many people with emetophobia who have gleaned their information from online groups and forums, anti-depressant medications are not "addictive." There can be withdrawal symptoms if someone stops taking their medication suddenly. Patients need to wean off slowly under the care and advice of a physician. "Addictive," or habit-forming, is an attribute of medications where the patient needs to take more and more of it to get the same effect over time. As a result, the patient eventually gets no benefit or very little but needs large quantities of the drug to stop becoming what addicts refer to as "sick" which means experiencing withdrawal symptoms. Withdrawing too suddenly from an addictive substance such as alcohol or opiates can cause intolerable withdrawal symptoms and even death. Patients with emetophobia should be given clear information about what "addictive" means if they are afraid of taking an anti-depressant for this reason.

### *Anxiolytics*

Anxiolytics, frequently benzodiazepines, are often prescribed to people with emetophobia for occasional use or for a "rescue" medication if they find themselves having a severe panic attack. We have had patients who were prescribed them for daily use in extreme cases, such as that of Tabitha in Chapter 2.

I (Anna) once had a prescription for lorazepam, "to take as needed for anxiety." I only used them for flying and going to the dentist after my emetophobia was successfully treated. I also took them whenever I had to go for a medical procedure after my breast cancer as I would panic then as well. Mammograms, X-rays, colonoscopies: they were all terrifying in some sort of PTSD-flashback kind of way.

Interestingly, once I used the lorazepam for flying a few times I no longer needed it. And I bravely got several hours' worth of cosmetic dentistry done with no lorazepam after a few years of having taken it for every check-up. Every few years now I ask my doctor for a prescription for four tablets just in case I need a random medical procedure. Benzodiazepines like lorazepam were meant to be used the way I was using them: *very* occasionally, and with the idea that eventually one could do the activity without them. There is nothing wrong with a crutch if one's leg is broken. Once the leg is healed, however, the crutch should be abandoned. We have found in our clinical work that most people with emetophobia who are prescribed tranquilizers use them as a safety behavior, so they should be discontinued under the supervision of their physician. Sometimes, they become part of a "safety kit," even if not used—carrying them around at all times should also be slowly discontinued. There are exceptions as in the case of Tabitha or another patient I had who took them twice daily before meals because she was underweight and terrified to eat.

### Antiobsessionals
Antiobsessional medications are often prescribed for people with emetophobia who exhibit strong OCD symptoms. Unfortunately, we find in our clinical practices that some people with emetophobia have a great deal of trouble with obsessive thoughts and OCD-type rituals who are prescribed anti-depressants, but not those which apparently work best as antiobsessionals.

Several antiobsessionals listed in the "Quick Psychiatric Reference to Medication®" in Preston et al. (2021) and which may be appropriate for patients with emetophobia are also SSRIs.

### Antipsychotics
According to Mind (2020) antipsychotic medication is mainly indicated for people with schizophrenia or brief psychotic breaks. However, it is often used now to help with bipolar disorder, severe depression, and sometimes severe anxiety. Many of our patients have been prescribed these medications. There are a number of them available, too numerous to list here.

## Conclusion
As we have stated, we are not physicians or pharmacists and so are not able to recommend any medical treatment to our patients. However, with the knowledge we have gleaned, we find that there are times when we recommend that one of our patients get a second opinion about their medication, especially if they have been prescribed something that seems out of the ordinary from what we have just discussed here. If patients have been prescribed the meds in question by a family physician, which is quite typical now, we might recommend they get

a referral to a psychiatrist to review them. I (Anna) find it beneficial to own a copy of the *Compendium of Pharmaceuticals and Specialties* (Canadian Pharmacists Association 2021) as well as the *Handbook of Clinical Psychopharmacology* (Preston et al. 2021) to refer to when a patient lists a medication they've been prescribed or are taking, especially if I am not familiar with it.

## — Chapter 9 —

# MAINTAINING GAINS

### Prognosis

People with emetophobia feel hopeless. Many believe that they can never get better or never live a normal life. Thousands will never have thought to look up "fear of vomiting" on the internet and so they feel completely alone. Parents, teachers, physicians, and therapists may have all communicated to them, in one way or another, that their fears are "silly," "ridiculous," and even "crazy," or that they've never heard of this fear or phobia. Millions more do not even have access to the internet. Many also believe that they have emetophobia worse than anyone else or that their symptoms are so severe that they can't possibly ever get over them, which can seem to justify their lack of hope.

Clinicians will want to assure their patients that emetophobia is a highly treatable disorder. New brain pathways can be created that take the patient from the stimulus (seeing someone vomit or feeling nauseous) to a new place of calm, confidence, and acceptance. Furthermore, patients need reassurance that if you cannot help them that you will refer them to someone else who can. We're convinced that after reading and digesting this book, provided you have training and experience with CBT, you will be able to treat them.

As long as the patient does not have comorbid conditions that complicate their emetophobia further, or is not willing to do the work, or runs out of money, then the prognosis is good. Unfortunately, in our experience many fall into this latter category, quitting therapy too soon or not really investing the time into the homework assignments sufficiently to recover from the disorder. However, as clinicians we're probably pretty used to this from people with all sorts of problems that brought them to therapy in the first place.

All of this being said, a course of CBT/ERP therapy in and of itself is not a psychological eraser of emetophobia. Despite the neuroplasticity of the brain there still remains a "superhighway" that goes from the stimulus to the amygdala, causing immediate irrational thoughts and panic. Over time, this superhighway begins to become less used and the longer, slower highway that goes from stimulus to a calm place of tolerance and acceptance gets stronger and comes to be stored in long-term memory. There is nothing scientific about this statement, but from my (Anna's) experience both personally and with all my patients with emetophobia, this process normally takes about two to three years, even though I only spend six months of that working with the patient.

Over these years, the patient will have to continue to work on exposure, continue to keep their safety behaviors eliminated and continue to use positive rather than anxious cognitions when thinking about nausea or illness in general (or if they have obsessive thoughts they must continue to leave them alone). They will also have to practice, each and every time they are triggered, to *take note* of their SUD level, ask themselves whether (or reassure themselves that) they can tolerate this number, and learn to carry on with their lives as if they were neurotypical and did not have the phobia. Usually after a couple of years of faithfully doing this, their emetophobia disappears into the background.

## Success Rate

No thanks to internet marketers who use slick web pages to advertise their "cures" for emetophobia, many prospective patients ask us our success rate. As psychiatrists, psychologists, and licensed psychotherapists, we are all bound to ethical standards. These standards forbid us from either asking for or receiving "reviews" from our current or former patients. Wannabe-therapists don't have this problem and so you see testimonials and reviews on their work all over the internet and none on ours. Of course, we all know that these reviews/testimonials can easily be paid for or simply created out of nothingness.

It's not like anyone's phone number or address is attached to them, as though they were general contractors or landscapers. All of this being said, success with a competent, educated, qualified and experienced clinician is mainly dependent upon the willingness and ability of the patient to do the work.

If insurance will not pay and the patient doesn't have money, then it's pretty tough to get better. Unfortunately, insurance rules both of our countries (Canada and the United States) when it comes to mental health. Perhaps one day governments will see the value in having a mentally healthy population. Physical ailments would be reduced, work productivity would increase, children would be healthier and less abused: the benefits are endless.

Any patient who is willing *and able* to work hard on their emetophobia and who takes the time to do the homework assignments and exercises will get better. This is especially true because we have spent a lot of time in this book talking about taking it slow, respecting the patient, and being compassionate with them. It's actually not that hard when you incorporate all three of these. Although it does get harder near the end, by that time the patient should have seen a good deal of progress and will be itching to see more. As well, they will have gained confidence that they are able to do the work and we are not interested in making them vomit.

Of the approximately 40 percent of patients that Anna has worked with who have committed themselves to the process and done all of the homework assignments, all of them have recovered from their emetophobia and are living normal lives. Many of the remaining 60 percent are much better than they were and can do some things they could never do before such as socialize more, eat in restaurants, and travel, even if they still have some anxiety. Many of our patients have met their goal of becoming pregnant, which is a delightful goal to have met. One woman was so thankful that she named her baby "Anna Sophia," after me! That was the most wonderful, touching bit of thanks I have ever had. Perhaps baby Anna Sophia will grow up and change the world. Even if she doesn't, I believe she will give her parents a lifetime of joy, and the children of people whom you treat will surely do the same.

## Common Obstacles
### Enabling/Accommodating

Sadly, one of the most common obstacles to people with emetophobia being successful in treatment and beyond is the well-meaning people who try to support them. Significant others may still enable them by shielding them from emotional triggers, such as lying to them when they or their children feel ill. What the patient needs by the time they finish treatment is to learn to deal with anyone who is sick. In fact, it's good practice and should be encouraged rather than discouraged.

### Identified Patient

Family members may become an obstacle also in subconscious ways. The family that has always dealt with all of its anxiety/stress by projecting it onto one member—usually a child but as adults it might be a sibling as well—will start to experience its own stress when the person with emetophobia gets better. Subconsciously and in no ways that are possible to be explained here, the family will try to get back its original homeostasis by pushing that person back into the role they always had, the "sick one," the one with the problems, or as Bateson et al. (1956) would dub them, the "identified patient."

The concept of an identified patient can be so subtle it is hard to pick up, or it can be astonishingly obvious. Just imagine for a moment that mom and dad have talked about Junior and what they're going to do with him and how they can help him for the past 15 or 20 years. He absorbs all of their time and energy. What are they going to talk about now? This situation is often repeated with adult patients when mother and sister spend all their time and energy and conversation worrying about and talking about the daughter/sister. Now she's doing quite well. What happens to all that energy? It is hard to describe it and it changes from family to family but the recovered person with emetophobia must look out for it or risk being pushed back into the phobia.

### Natural Avoidance

The third thing that affects outcome is the recovered patient *not* running into any situations around vomiting. The worst obstacle to continued progress would be to live a rather sheltered life, not watch movies, and not socialize with other people, even family. I live in the suburbs and did not see vomit on a sidewalk for about 30 years. But those who live in the city, particularly near bars, may see it at least once a week. It would be far better for the recovered person with emetophobia to live in the city, to have children, to go to lots of kids' events, etc., but this is not always possible. Continued avoidance of feared situations and/or picking up the use of safety behaviors again is a great obstacle to a good prognosis. Often when we see patients again for a check-up session after a few years because their phobia has "come back," we discover after a subsequent assessment that they have started avoiding or using safety behaviors again. Once reminded of this, they can begin to give them up once more and go back to facing the situations they would have normally avoided.

I (David) recommend to my child patients that they practice exposure for at least six months after they finish treatment. I suggest every other week that they look at a variety of the types of exposures we have covered, or even better, to go find them online. I suggest this even though they might be bored of them. It will help reinforce that they are not afraid. Craske et al. (2014) describe it as "occasional reinforced extinction." I also suggest they take a "ferocious" attitude to any hint of returning to a safety behavior. They need to be seriously aggressive to *not* do that. I also recommend they immediately seek treatment if they relapse as the second round is generally much quicker if they address it as soon as possible.

## Group Therapy

I (Anna) have been very fortunate and honored to have been included in a group therapy program begun by Dr David Kosins, psychologist, from Seattle, Washington, USA. Dr Kosins treats many forms of anxiety disorders and OCD. He eventually began holding a group for people with phobias. A couple of people with blood-injection phobia and illness anxiety were in the group, but the rest were people with emetophobia. Soon it became a group solely for people with emetophobia. It was great to see them teaming up with one another to do continued exposure work such as visiting hospital ER waiting rooms. I visited the group in Seattle, just a couple of hours from my home in Vancouver. Once Covid-19 hit we all began meeting on Zoom.

Members of the group share stories of their progress and the exposures they've been doing, and receive support and encouragement from other group members and the clinicians. This is a wonderful way to continue to progress with one's recovery from emetophobia.

## Family Support

Formerly listed as a possible obstacle to continued recovery, family support can nevertheless be an important component of continued recovery. Contrary to popular belief, having a family member recover from emetophobia can be stressful on the family unit. Ideally, a course of family or at least couples therapy would be recommended. It is doubtful that families would immediately see the necessity for this, however. Nevertheless, individual family members such as parents or significant others can support the newly recovered person with emetophobia in several important ways.

### Patience

Love, compassion, understanding, and patience are important as the family member recovers. Recovery will not be all at once and especially not after 20 sessions of therapy. It may take a couple of years before the patient feels as though emetophobia is behind them. Meanwhile, there will still be times when the person is anxious or when they appear to have slid back into the phobia. If family members become anxious, start worrying, or worse, become frustrated and angry with the patient, it will make them worse instead of continuing to aid in their progress.

### Designated Support Person

With adults, a designated support person such as a significant other can be incredibly helpful with a bit of training. I (Anna) like to meet with the support person and the patient after about six or eight sessions to let them know how they can best help. I teach them the STAR plan and let them know that if their loved one with emetophobia begins to panic, it's their job to remind them of the plan. "Just ask how anxious they are, 0–10" I will say. As a follow-up to the answer, ask "can you tolerate that?" I tell them to be prepared for the wrath of hell to rain down upon them and not to take it personally. It is only the "fight" instinct in the "fight-or-flight" response. I coach them not to remind their loved one of any other parts of the plan or they will probably just annoy them. Besides, their loved one is a grown-up and is responsible for getting through this themselves, even without any support.

Support persons must be careful not to enable their loved ones, no matter how angry they might become. Again, the responsibility for their own healing is theirs and theirs alone. If they want you to burn the chicken, don't do it. If they ask you to partake in silly things such as taking a shower before you move the clothes from the washer to the dryer, don't do that either. Behave normally, as you would if you were not living with a person with emetophobia. Requests for comfort such as lying down with the anxious person or rubbing their back when they're anxious should be refused. This sounds cold and unfeeling, but it is actually deeply loving because it helps the anxious person cope with their anxiety in the long run.

Support persons should not reassure their loved ones about anything related to the phobia and they should also not answer any question more than once. While it is important to be patient and compassionate, offering reassurance is the worst way to do that. Seeking reassurance is a symptom of the disorder, so offering it only continues the phobia. I remember a patient who used to always ask her husband if he thought the leftover rice would make her sick. Once they both met with me and agreed that he would not answer that question anymore, the very next week she asked him, "do you think this rice is still okay to eat?" and without thinking he answered her. I found out about this when the patient herself told me that she did it!

### Autonomy

Family members must allow the patient to solve their own problems. This is true whether or not the problem seems related to emetophobia. People recovering from emetophobia have spent a lot of time in their life dependent upon others to "help them" because of their phobia. This may have involved taking them places, making excuses for them, cooking the chicken until it's dried out, making phone calls, etc. As a result, the person with emetophobia becomes unable or less able to solve problems in general, because their preferred method is to look to someone else. With adolescents this is the most challenging, but some young adults and even older adults have never solved a problem on their own and may react with anger or despair when encouraged to do so. Staying the course and refusing to bail them out will be very important to their eventual full recovery.

## Personal Work

Recovering and recovered people with emetophobia should be encouraged to continue their personal work in individual therapy, perhaps even with a different modality than CBT, such as ACT, emotion-focused, or EMDR. For those patients who can afford to pay for a long course of private therapy, this is ideal. The more therapy we have the more we can address all the underlying issues that may have led to the phobia in the first place.

— *Chapter 10* —

# FURTHER RESEARCH

As mentioned, emetophobia, relative to its terrible personal impact, is strikingly under-researched. This chapter examines research exigencies from the existing literature as well as our experience to suggest possible future studies, assessment instruments, and clinical resources. We sincerely hope that this book will also inspire those interested in research to work on this very serious disorder which affects millions of people.

## OCD

An important initial piece of research on OCD and emetophobia is the study done by Veale, Hennig, and Gledhill (2015). More is being learned all the time about OCD, which is evident by its new section in the DSM-5. As we noted in Chapter 3 about comorbid conditions, emetophobia is almost always comorbid with OCD in some form, often not seemingly related to the emetophobia. Veale et al. (2015) proposed that emetophobia may in fact be a newly discovered subset of OCD. If it is, then research and treatments need to be targeted specifically in this area of study.

While we "invented" the Emet-OCD continuum diagram and came up with certain conclusions regarding it, more research needs to be done in this area. It would be helpful if research were aimed at placing those diagnosed with emetophobia somewhere on the continuum and studying whether cognitive restructuring was helpful for those low on the OCD end, or whether all people with SPOV actually sit high on the OCD continuum, meaning that they have obsessive thoughts which cannot be controlled or countered.

## Assessment

While we are incredibly appreciative of the two assessment instruments created for emetophobia as diagnostic tools, there has not yet been sufficient research to determine if lower scores are indicative of successful treatment. Boschen et al. (2013) indicated that more research on the EmetQ-13 is needed.

## Efficacy of Treatment Modalities

We would be very interested to see research done on various treatment methods and protocols specifically for emetophobia. For example, studies could compare traditional CBT/ERP using desensitization methods to calm or control anxiety with newer modalities which stress tolerance and acceptance of anxiety.

In the UK, clinicians trained and licensed in hypnosis are more popular than in North America or Australia. Ritow (1979) and McKenzie (1994) have studied hypnosis for emetophobia and claim success with this modality. Further research is needed in the form of randomized controlled trials (RCTs) comparing the efficacy of hypnosis with CBT/ERP. Similar RCTs comparing EMDR with CBT/ERP for emetophobia would also be helpful.

Since Philips (1985) there has only been one further study of CBT for emetophobia, conducted by Riddle-Walker et al. (2016), which was the first (and so far, the only) RCT on emetophobia to evaluate a protocol for CBT compared with a waitlist. Further high-quality RCTs with larger sample sizes in this area are imperative.

## Anna and David

Anna would like to see research evaluating attachment styles for children with SPOV as compared to a control group. This might help us to learn more about why SPOV arises so that we could create interventions and treatments for children so that SPOV does not continue into adulthood. Research could also be aimed at evaluating the health of families with children with SPOV.

David would like to see a good diagnostic instrument for children, and RCTs on treatment modalities for children and adolescents. Ongoing research is being done on PANDAS, particularly around OCD.

To date no research has been targeted toward PANDAS and emeto-phobia, however, which would be immensely helpful for pediatricians and pediatric clinicians.

## Researchers' Suggestions

Those who have already published studies on emetophobia have indi-cated the following areas for further study:

- Compare treatment modalities in an RCT (Riddle-Walker et al. 2016).
- Prevalence of SPOV in adolescents (Kannappan and Middleman 2020).
- More research on SPOV and adolescents in general (Fix, Proc-tor, and Gray 2016).
- Evaluate the effectiveness of imagery re-scripting for SPOV (Keyes et al. 2020).
- Published treatment studies, randomized controlled trials and larger sample sizes. High-quality RCTs for effectiveness of psychological treatments (Keyes, Gilpin, and Veale 2018).
- Comparison of treatment modalities for efficacy (Dosanjh, Fleisher, and Sam 2017).
- Is exposure to vomit necessary? Is interoceptive exposure nec-essary? Or is gradual exposure to avoided situations and giving up safety behaviors enough? (Van Hout and Bouman 2011).
- Study the "multifarious" and sometimes OCD-like symptom-ology of SPOV (Simons and Vloet 2018).
- Examine fear and avoidance of nausea in SPOV. Do they main-tain the disorder? (Höller et al. 2013).
- More studies on etiology, epidemiology, clinical picture, and treatments (Faye et al. 2013).
- Better conceptual understanding of SPOV; assess efficacy of treatments and refine their usage (Maack, Deacon, and Zhao 2013).
- Further study on emetophobia and control (Davidson, Boyle, and Lauchlan 2007).
- Are there subgroups of patients with SPOV? (Van Overveld et al. 2008).

- Why does emetophobia affect more women than men, even when controlling for anxiety in general? (David Veale in Christie 2021).

## Conclusion

Emetophobia is under-researched, misunderstood, and often misdiagnosed. As I (Anna) write this conclusion today, in June of 2022, typing "emetophobia" into a Google Scholar search yields 880 results. "Obsessive compulsive disorder" yields 652,000. We need more research.

Most physicians (even psychiatrists), therapists, counselors, and teachers have still never heard of emetophobia, or know of it and belittle it. As a result, parents of children with emetophobia also brush off their child's (severe) phobia as "silly" or "ridiculous." All this ignorance about emetophobia leads those who have it to despair and lose hope.

When I suffered from emetophobia I was bounced around from clinician to clinician, all of whom shook their heads. I became more and more discouraged, believing that I was probably the only person who feared vomiting in the world. And yet I never gave up hope that there was a way to overcome it. Eventually I thanked God for the dawn of the information age. I first found the name for my disorder, and then a community of others with the same phobia in an online forum. People are more likely to look on Facebook today for groups of people like themselves, and it does not disappoint. There are at least ten groups on Facebook for emetophobia, including for mothers, those who only fear others, and so on. There are support groups where one can go and ask for reassurance (the worst kind) and get it, and there are "no panic" groups where you can discuss recovery and triumphs. Most groups have members censor any word that could possibly be triggering; two groups do not. There are also pages on Facebook with current research and information. Many people with emetophobia write blogs. Lots of clinicians and anxiety disorder centers have web pages. Like the reincarnation of the radio age, young people today are into podcasts. Besides my own there are some others now on emetophobia. There are also books, magazine articles, blogs, research studies, and even a designated charity for emetophobia.

Now that you have read this book, you will be another beacon of hope for at least one person with emetophobia. The more people you speak to about the disorder (colleagues, friends, family), the more the information about emetophobia will spread exponentially; shame and guilt around having the disorder will fade, and at last those who develop a severe fear of vomiting will have healing and hope.

## ANNA'S STORY—PART 10

In 2010 my daughter, Alex, and I both caught a nasty case of norovirus when I was moving her to another province. We were together in her one-bedroom, one-bathroom basement apartment. One bathroom = not good! The day after, as we sat at the kitchen table sipping Gatorade and sort of musing about the whole experience, it was as if a light bulb went on for Alex and she said, "Mom, you weren't scared at all."

"Oh yeah," I said. "Huh."

And that was that.

# Resources

## Emetophobia Charity

Founded and run by academic researchers, this charity seeks donations for further research to be done on emetophobia. The website at www.emetaction.org has general information about emetophobia as well as a blog.

## Books

Cacciatore, M. (2018) *When a Child's Anxiety Takes Over: A Mother's Struggle to Save her Child from Emetophobia, Second Edition*. Scotts Valley, CA: CreateSpace Independent Publishing.

Goodman, K. (2020) *The Emetophobia Manual: Free Yourself from the Fear of Vomit and Reclaim Your Life*. Porter Ranch, CA: Anxiety & OCD Treatment of the Valley.

Huebner, D. (2022) *Facing Mighty Fears about Throwing Up, Illustrated Edition* (Dr Dawn's Mini Books about Mighty Fears). London: Jessica Kingsley Publishers.

Keyes, A., and Veale, D. (2021) *Free Yourself from Emetophobia: A CBT Self-Help Guide for a Fear of Vomiting*. London: Jessica Kingsley Publishers.

Lovitz, D., and Yusko, D. (2021) *Gag Reflections: Conquering a Fear of Vomit through Exposure Therapy*. Jefferson, NC: Toplight Books.

Roche, J. (2023) *Tummy Troubles: Gretchen Faces Her Fear of Throwing Up*. Washington, DC: American Psychological Association.

Russ, D. (2022) *Emetophobia! The Ultimate Kids' Guide, 2nd edition* [E-book]. Charlotte, NC: Skyline Publishing.

Watkins, S. (2018) *Scared to Be Sick: A Self-Help Workbook for Emetophobia*. London: Independent Publishing Network.

## Podcasts
Emetophobia Help with Anna Christie.
The Emetophobia Podcast (Casey Vandemark).
Living Life with Emetophobia (Brooke & Maddie).

## Blogs
Emetophobia Help: https://emetophobiahelp.org/blog
Emetophobia Resources: www.emetophobia.net
David Veale Blog: www.veale.co.uk/blog
Turnaround Anxiety: www.turnaroundanxiety.com/blog

## Reviews
Anna reviews books and programs on emetophobia: https://emetophobia-help.org/reviews
@emetophobiareview on Instagram and https://emetophobiareview.tumblr.com review movies and TV shows for vomit content.

## Social Media
Information and support groups can be found on virtually every social media platform. Anna has a presence on Facebook with a public information page "Emetophobia Help" and as moderator of the private group "Emetophobia NO PANIC." She posts weekly to most other social media platforms such as Instagram, Twitter, and Reddit. There are support groups on every platform, many of which are members asking for reassurance that they won't vomit or for information about safety behaviors. Patients should probably be cautioned away from these types of groups or asked to give them up when they give up other safety behaviors. Some pages on social media review movies and TV shows to warn people with emetophobia away, but these can be turned around to use as exposures.

## Websites

Our new website featuring resources for therapists treating emetophobia in adults and children: www.emetophobia.net

Anna's website with free information, a therapist list, and other help for people with emetophobia: www.emetophobiahelp.org

David's websites for helping children with anxiety: www.turnaroundanxiety.com

A community-oriented website with information about emetophobia including content and discussion by community members: www.stuffthatworks.health/emetophobia

## YouTube Channels

Dr David Veale: www.youtube.com/c/DrDavidVeale

EmetophobiaHelp: www.youtube.com/user/EmetophobiaHelp

Emetophobia Resources: www.youtube.com/@emetophobiaresources

— *Appendix 2* —

# Research Studies on Emetophobia in Chronological Order

Compiled by Anna S. Christie. The type of study is described only if not evident by the title or publication.

| Year | Article | Type |
|------|---------|------|
| 1974 | Wijesinghe, B. "A vomiting phobia overcome by one session of flooding with hypnosis." *Journal of Behavior Therapy and Experimental Psychiatry.* | Case study (flooding) |
| 1979 | Ritow, J.K. "Brief treatment of a vomiting phobia." *American Journal of Clinical Hypnosis.* | Case study (hypnosis) |
| 1983 | McFadyen, M., and Wyness, J. "You don't have to be sick to be a behaviour therapist but it can help! Treatment of a 'vomit' phobia." *Behavioural Psychotherapy.* | Case study (exposure using simulation) |
| 1984 | Klonoff, E.A., Knell, S.M., and Janata, J.W. "Fear of nausea and vomiting: The interaction among psychosocial stressors, development transitions, and adventitious reinforcement." *Journal of Clinical Child Psychology.* | Theoretical review |
| 1985 | Philips, H. "Return of fear in the treatment of a fear of vomiting." *Behaviour Research and Therapy.* | (Group CBT/ ERP) |

| 1990 | Manassis, K., and Kalman, E. "Anorexia resulting from fear of vomiting in four adolescent girls." *The Canadian Journal of Psychiatry.* | |
| 1993 | Herman, D.S., Rozensky, R.H., and Mineka, S. "Cognitive behavioral therapy for panic disorder with a primary fear of vomiting: Conceptual and treatment issues." *Proceedings for Association for Advancement of Behaviour Therapy.* | |
| 1994 | de Jongh, A., and ten Broeke, E. "Notable changes after one session of eye movement desensitization and reprocessing: A case of fear of nausea and vomiting." *Directieve Therapie.* | Case study—Netherlands (EMDR) |
| 1994 | McKenzie, S. "Hypnotherapy for vomiting phobia in a 40-year-old woman." *Contemporary Hypnosis.* | Case study (hypnosis) |
| 2001 | Lipsitz, J.D., Fyer, A.J., Paterniti, A., and Klein, D.F. "Emetophobia: Preliminary results of an internet survey." *Depression & Anxiety.* | Internet survey |
| 2003 | Dattilio, F.M. "Emetic exposure and desensitization procedures in the reduction of nausea and a fear of emesis." *Clinical Case Studies.* | Case study (exposure/desensitization using ipecac) |
| 2005 | Moran, D.J., and O'Brien, R.M. "Competence imagery: A case study treating emetophobia." *Psychological Reports.* | |
| 2006 | Veale, D., and Lambrou, C. "The psychopathology of vomit phobia." *Behavioural and Cognitive Psychotherapy.* | |
| 2006 | Baeyens, C., and Philippot, P. "L'émétophobie: Un cas particulier de phobie intéroceptive? [Emetophobia: A special case of interoceptive phobia?]." *Revue Francophone de Clinique Comportementale et Cognitive.* | Theoretical review—French |
| 2006 | Whitton, S.W., Luiselli, J.K., and Donaldson, D.L. "Cognitive-behavioral treatment of generalized anxiety." *Clinical Case Studies.* | (Emetophobia misdiagnosed as GAD) |

*cont.*

| Year | Article | Type |
|------|---------|------|
| 2007 | Davidson, A.L., Boyle, C., and Lauchlan, F. "Scared to lose control? General and health locus of control in females with a phobia of vomiting." *Journal of Clinical Psychology*. | |
| 2007 | Boschen, M.J. "Reconceptualizing emetophobia: A cognitive–behavioral formulation and research agenda." *Journal of Anxiety Disorders*. | |
| 2008 | Van Overveld, M., De Jong, P.J., Peters, M.L., Van Hout, W.J., and Bouman, T.K. "An internet-based study on the relation between disgust sensitivity and emetophobia." *Journal of Anxiety Disorders*. | |
| 2009 | Hunter, P.V., and Antony, M.M. "Cognitive-behavioral treatment of emetophobia: The role of interoceptive exposure." *Cognitive and Behavioral Practice*. | Case study |
| 2009 | Veale, D. "Cognitive behaviour therapy for a specific phobia of vomiting." *The Cognitive Behaviour Therapist*. | |
| 2010 | Graziano, P.A., Callueng, C.M., and Geffken, G.R. "Cognitive-behavioral treatment of an 11-year-old male presenting with emetophobia: A case study." *Clinical Case Studies*. | |
| 2010 | Pearson, M.R. "Characteristics, correlates, and experiences of emetophobia: An exploratory study." Theses and dissertations. Paper 1480. | Doctoral dissertation |
| 2011 | Leite, C.E.P., Vicentini, H.C., Neves, J.D.S., and Torres, A.R. "Emetofobia: Revisão crítica sobre um transtorno pouco estudado. [Emetophobia: A Critical Review of an Understudied Disorder.]" *Jornal Brasileiro de Psiquiatria*. | Critical review—Brazil |
| 2011 | Vandereycken, W. "Media hype, diagnostic fad or genuine disorder? Professionals' opinions about night eating syndrome, orthorexia, muscle dysmorphia, and emetophobia." *Eating Disorders*. | |

| 2011 | Williams, K.E., Field, D.G., Riegel, K., and Paul, C. "Brief, intensive behavioral treatment of food refusal secondary to emetophobia." *Clinical Case Studies.* | |
|------|---------|---------|
| 2011 | Kobori, O. "Cognitive therapy for vomit phobia: A case report." *Asia Pacific Journal of Counselling and Psychotherapy.* | Case study— Japanese (cognitive therapy) |
| 2011 | Van Hout, W.J., and Bouman, T.K. "Clinical features, prevalence and psychiatric complaints in subjects with fear of vomiting." *Clinical Psychology and Psychotherapy.* | Survey (Dutch) |
| 2012 | Veale, D., Costa, A., Murphy, P., and Ellison, N. "Abnormal eating behaviour in people with a specific phobia of vomiting (emetophobia)." *European Eating Disorders Review.* | |
| 2012 | Price, K., Veale, D., and Brewin, C.R. "Intrusive imagery in people with a specific phobia of vomiting." *Journal of Behavior Therapy and Experimental Psychiatry.* | |
| 2012 | de Jongh, A. "Treatment of a woman with emetophobia: A trauma focused approach." *Mental Illness.* | |
| 2013 | Kerr, C. "TA treatment of emetophobia: A hermeneutic single-case efficacy design study—'Peter.'" *International Journal of Transactional Analysis Research and Practice.* | |
| 2013 | Faye, A., Gawande, S., Tadke, R., Kirpekar, V., and Bhave, S. "Emetophobia: A fear of vomiting." *Indian Journal of Psychiatry.* | |
| 2013 | Veale, D., Ellison, N., Boschen, M.J., Costa, A., et al. "Development of an inventory to measure specific phobia of vomiting (emetophobia)." *Cognitive Therapy Research.* | |
| 2013 | Maack, D.J., Deacon, B.J., and Zhao, M. "Exposure therapy for emetophobia: A case study with three-year follow-up." *Journal of Anxiety Disorders.* | |

*cont.*

| Year | Article | Type |
|------|---------|------|
| 2013 | Boschen, M.J., Veale, D., Ellison, N., and Reddell, T. "The emetophobia questionnaire (EmetQ-13): Psychometric validation of a measure of specific phobia of vomiting (emetophobia)." *Journal of Anxiety Disorders*. | |
| 2013 | Höller, Y., Overveld, M.V., Jutglar, H., and Trinka, E. "Nausea in specific phobia of vomiting." *Behavioral Science*. | Internet survey (German) |
| 2014 | Zhao, M. "Toward a conceptualization of emetophobia: Examining intolerance of uncertainty as a unique predictor of symptoms." *Electronic Theses and Dissertations*. | Master's thesis |
| 2014 | Veale, D., Murphy, P., Ellison, N., Kanakam, N., and Costa, A. "Autobiographical memories of vomiting in people with a specific phobia of vomiting (emetophobia)." *Journal of Behavior Therapy and Experimental Psychiatry*. | |
| 2014 | Snæbjarnardóttir, K., and Sigurðsson, E. "Emetophobia: Sjúklegur ótti við uppköst og ógleði [Emetophobia: morbid fear of vomiting and nausea]." *Læknablaðið*. | Case study—Iceland |
| 2015 | Benoit, J-P. "Quand la phobie s'empare du corps: À propos de l'émétophobie [When phobia takes hold of the body: about emetophobia]." *Enfances & Psy*. | Overview— French |
| 2015 | Wu, M.S., Rudy, B.M., Arnold, E.B., and Storch, E.A. "Phenomenology, clinical correlates, and impairment in emetophobia." *Journal of Cognitive Psychotherapy*. | |
| 2015 | Ahlen, J., Edberg, E., Di Schiena, M., and Bergström, J. "Cognitive behavioural group therapy for emetophobia: An open study in a psychiatric setting." *Clinical Psychologist*. | |
| 2015 | Veale, D., Hennig, C., and Gledhill, L. "Is a specific phobia of vomiting part of the obsessive compulsive and related disorders?" *Journal of Obsessive-Compulsive and Related Disorders*. | |

| 2015 | Brunner, J. "Emetophobie bei einem jungen Mann. [Emetophobia in a young man]." *Psychotherapeut.* | Case study—German |
|------|--------------------------------------------------------------------------------------------------------------------------------------------------------------------------|------------------------------------------|
| 2016 | Riddle-Walker, L., Veale, D., Chapman, C., Ogle, F. *et al.* "Cognitive behaviour therapy for specific phobia of vomiting (emetophobia): A pilot randomized controlled trial." *Journal of Anxiety Disorders.* | Randomized controlled trial |
| 2016 | Fix, R.L., Proctor, K.B., and Gray, W.N. "Treating emetophobia and panic symptoms in an adolescent female." *Clinical Case Studies.* | Case study (adolescent: Rx + CBT) |
| 2016 | Sykes, M., Boschen, M.J., and Conlon, E.G. "Comorbidity in emetophobia (specific phobia of vomiting)." *Clinical Psychology and Psychotherapy.* | |
| 2016 | Verwoerd, J., Van Hout, W.J., and De Jong, P.J. "Disgust- and anxiety-based emotional reasoning in non-clinical fear of vomiting." *Journal of Behavior Therapy and Experimental Psychiatry.* | |
| 2016 | Wu, M.S., Selles, R.R., Novoa, J.C., Zepeda, R., et al. "Examination of the phenomenology and clinical correlates of emetophobia in a sample of Salvadorian youths." *Child Psychiatry and Human Development.* | |
| 2016 | Paulus, D.J., and Norton, P.J. "Purging anxiety: A case study of transdiagnostic CBT for a complex fear of vomiting (emetophobia)." *Cognitive and Behavioral Practice.* | Case study |
| 2016 | Van Hout, W., and Bouman, T. "Imagery and core beliefs in fear of vomiting." 8th World Congress of Behavioural and Cognitive Therapies, Melbourne, Australia. | Convention presentation (Australia) |
| 2017 | Dosanjh, S., Fleisher, W., and Sam, D. (2017) "I think I'm going to be sick: An eight-year-old boy with emetophobia and secondary food restriction." *Journal of the Canadian Academy of Child and Adolescent Psychiatry.* | Case study |

*cont.*

| Year | Article | Type |
|------|---------|------|
| 2017 | Gormez, V., Meral, Y., and Orengul, A. "Emetophobia (specific phobia of vomiting): Its relationship with anxiety-related disorders and cognitive behavioral therapeutic approach." *Journal of Cognitive-Behavioral Psychotherapy and Research*. | Theoretical review—Istanbul, Turkey |
| 2017 | Roy, D. "Emetophobia (a specific phobia of vomiting): A case study." *European Psychiatry*. | |
| 2017 | Maertens, C., Couturier, J., Grant, C., and Johnson, N. "Fear of vomiting and low body weight in two pediatric patients: diagnostic challenges." *Journal of the Canadian Academy of Child and Adolescent Psychiatry*. | |
| 2017 | Veale, D., and Keyes, A. "Atypical eating disorders and specific phobia of vomiting: Clinical presentation and treatment approaches." In L.K. Anderson, S.B. Murray, and W.H. Kaye (eds) *Clinical Handbook of Complex and Atypical Eating Disorders*. Oxford University Press. | |
| 2018 | Dargis, M., and Burk, L. "A transdiagnostic approach to the treatment of emetophobia: A single case study." *Clinical Case Studies*. | |
| 2018 | Liebenberg, A., and Dos Santos, M. "Health-related subjective well-being with emetophobia." *Journal of Psychology in Africa*. | Assessment—African |
| 2018 | Simons, M., and Vloet, T.D. "Emetophobia—A metacognitive therapeutic approach for an overlooked disorder." *Zeitschrift für Kinder- und Jugendpsychiatrie und Psychotherapie*. | Case study—Germany |
| 2018 | Nakamura, M., and Kitanishi, K. "Morita therapy for the treatment of emetophobia: A case report." *Asia-Pacific Psychiatry*. | Case study—Japan |

| | | |
|---|---|---|
| 2018 | Bogusch, L.M., Moeller, M.T., and O'Brien, W.H. "Case study of acceptance and commitment therapy and functional analysis for emetophobia." *Clinical Case Studies*. | |
| 2018 | Keyes, A., Gilpin, H.R., and Veale, D. "Phenomenology, epidemiology, co-morbidity and treatment of a specific phobia of vomiting: A systematic review of an understudied disorder." *Clinical Psychology Review*. | Systematic review |
| 2018 | Maack, D.J., Ebesutani, C., and Smitherman, T.A. "Psychometric investigation of the specific phobia of vomiting inventory: A new factor model." *International Journal of Methods in Psychiatric Research*. | |
| 2019 | Petell, J.A. "Behavioral similarities and differences among symptoms of emetophobia, disordered eating, and disgust." Electronic Theses and Dissertations. 1937. | Master's thesis |
| 2019 | Salgado, M.E. "Someone could be sick: Cognitive behaviour therapy for a specific phobia of vomiting (emetophobia): A case study." *Revista Argentina de Clinica Psicologica*. | Argentina |
| 2019 | Mitamura, T. "Case study of clinical behavior analysis for a 20-year-old patient with emetophobia." *Clinical Case Studies*. | |
| 2020 | Kannappan, A., and Middleman, A.B. "Emetophobia: A case of nausea leading to dehydration in an adolescent female." *SAGE Open Medical Case Reports*. | |
| 2020 | Mircea, M.M. "Employing long short-term memory networks in trigger detection for emetophobia." *Studia Universitatis Babeş-Bolyai Informatica*. | Romania— studied and created an API and Chrome extension to censor emetophobia-triggering words. |

*cont.*

| Year | Article | Type |
|------|---------|------|
| 2020 | Keyes, A., Veale, A., Foster, C., and Veale, D. "Time intensive cognitive behavioural therapy for a specific phobia of vomiting: A single case experimental design." *Journal of Behavior Therapy and Experimental Psychiatry.* | |
| 2022 | Zickgraf, H.F., Loftus, P., Gibbons, B., Cohen, L.C., and Hunt, M.G. "If I could survive without eating, it would be a huge relief: Development and initial validation of the Fear of Food Questionnaire." *Appetite.* | Assessment instrument |
| 2022 | Orme, K., Challacombe, F., and Roxborough, A. "Specific fear of vomiting (SPOV) in early parenthood: Assessment and treatment considerations with two illustrative cases." *The Cognitive Behaviour Therapist.* | |

# Diagnostic Instruments

## SPOVI

The SPOVI (Veale et al. 2013a) is a 14-item questionnaire "designed to measure the frequency of key cognitive processes and behaviors in emetophobia" (David Veale, personal communication, June 3, 2022). It is scored on a Likert scale where 0 = "not at all" and 4 = "all the time," with a range of 0 to 56. A score of 10 or more is considered positive for emetophobia. The two subscales include checking/scanning for threats and avoidance behaviors, each with seven items.

Instructions: Please circle the number that best describes how your fear of vomiting has affected you over the past week, including today.

| 0 | 1 | 2 | 3 | 4 |
|---|---|---|---|---|
| Not at All | A Little | Often | A Lot | All the Time |

| | | | | | | |
|---|---|---|---|---|---|---|
| 1 | I have been avoiding adults or children because of my fear of vomiting | 0 | 1 | 2 | 3 | 4 |
| 2 | I have been avoiding objects that other people have touched because of my fear of vomiting | 0 | 1 | 2 | 3 | 4 |

*cont.*

| 3 | I have been avoiding situations or activities because of my fear of vomiting | 0 | 1 | 2 | 3 | 4 |
|---|---|---|---|---|---|---|
| 4 | I have been looking at others to see if they may be ill and vomiting | 0 | 1 | 2 | 3 | 4 |
| 5 | I have escaped from situations because I am afraid I or others may vomit | 0 | 1 | 2 | 3 | 4 |
| 6 | I have been restricting the amount or type of food I eat or alcohol I drink because of my fear of vomiting | 0 | 1 | 2 | 3 | 4 |
| 7 | I have been trying to avoid or control any thoughts or images about vomiting | 0 | 1 | 2 | 3 | 4 |
| 8 | I have been feeling nauseous | 0 | 1 | 2 | 3 | 4 |
| 9 | If I think I am going to vomit, I do something to try to stop myself from vomiting | 0 | 1 | 2 | 3 | 4 |
| 10 | I have been trying to find reasons to explain why I feel nauseous | 0 | 1 | 2 | 3 | 4 |
| 11 | I have been focused on whether I feel ill and may vomit, rather than on my surroundings | 0 | 1 | 2 | 3 | 4 |
| 12 | I have been worrying about myself or others vomiting | 0 | 1 | 2 | 3 | 4 |

| 13 | I have been thinking about how to stop myself or others from vomiting | 0 | 1 | 2 | 3 | 4 |
|----|------------------------------------------------------------------------|---|---|---|---|---|
| 14 | I have been seeking reassurance that I or others will not be ill and vomit | 0 | 1 | 2 | 3 | 4 |
| **TOTAL** | | | | | | |

*Source: Veale et al. (2013a). Used with permission.*

# EMETQ-13[1]

EmetQ-13 is a 13-item inventory and a three-factor structure. It is meant to measure the severity of symptoms. The range of scores is 13 to 65. Any score above 22 is normally a diagnosis of emetophobia. This instrument also has three subscales:

- Items 1–6 indicate avoidance of travel and places where no help is available.
- Items 7–9 indicate how dangerous the patient believes exposure to vomit is.
- Items 10–13 indicate avoiding other people who may vomit.

**EmetQ-13**

Instructions: The following questionnaire is designed to measure the severity of fear of vomiting over the past week, including today. Please read each question carefully and, on the 1 to 5 scale, indicate your response by circling the appropriate number next to each question.

| 1 | 2 | 3 | 4 | 5 |
|---|---|---|---|---|
| Strongly Disagree | Disagree | Unsure | Agree | Strongly Agree |

---

1   From David Veale, personal correspondence, June 3, 2022

| 1 | I avoid air travel because I may become nauseous/vomit | 1 | 2 | 3 | 4 | 5 |
|---|---|---|---|---|---|---|
| 2 | I avoid other forms of transport because I may become nauseous/vomit | 1 | 2 | 3 | 4 | 5 |
| 3 | I avoid sea travel (boats, etc.) because I may become nauseous/vomit | 1 | 2 | 3 | 4 | 5 |
| 4 | I avoid places where there are no facilities to cater if I become nauseous/vomit | 1 | 2 | 3 | 4 | 5 |
| 5 | I avoid places where there is no medical attention, because I may become nauseous/vomit | 1 | 2 | 3 | 4 | 5 |
| 6 | I avoid fast-moving activities like rides at the theme park, because I may vomit | 1 | 2 | 3 | 4 | 5 |
| 7 | If I see vomit, I may be sick myself | 1 | 2 | 3 | 4 | 5 |
| 8 | If I smell vomit, I may be sick myself | 1 | 2 | 3 | 4 | 5 |
| 9 | Exposure to vomit can cause sickness and/or illness | 1 | 2 | 3 | 4 | 5 |
| 10 | I avoid adults who may be likely to vomit | 1 | 2 | 3 | 4 | 5 |
| 11 | I avoid children who may be likely to vomit | 1 | 2 | 3 | 4 | 5 |
| 12 | I avoid places where others may vomit | 1 | 2 | 3 | 4 | 5 |
| 13 | I notice physical anxiety symptoms when exposed to vomit | 1 | 2 | 3 | 4 | 5 |
| **TOTAL** | | | | | | |

*Source: Boschen et al. (2013). Used with permission.*

# References

Abramowitz, J.S., Deacon, B.J., and Whiteside, S.P.H. (2019) *Exposure Therapy for Anxiety, Second Edition*. New York: Guilford Press.

Ahlen, J., Edberg, E., Di Schiena, M., and Bergström, J. (2015) "Cognitive behavioural group therapy for emetophobia: An open study in a psychiatric setting." *Clinical Psychologist 19*, 2, 96–104.

American Partnership for Esophageal Disorders (APFED) (2022) *EoE*. Accessed on 30/4/22 at https://apfed.org/about-ead/egids/eoe

American Psychiatric Association (2022) *Diagnostic and Statistical Manual of Mental Disorders, Fifth Edition, Text Revision: DSM-5-TR*. Washington, DC: American Psychiatric Association Press.

Bastian, R. (2022). *Cricopharyngeus Spasm and What to Do About It*. Laryngopedia. Accessed on 28/9/22 at https://laryngopedia.com/cricopharyngeus-spasm-and-what-to-do-about-it

Bateson, G., Jackson, D.D., Haley, J., and Weakland, J. (1956) "Toward a theory of schizophrenia." *Behavioral Science 1*, 4, 251–264.

Becker, E.S., Rinck, M., Türke, V., Kause, P., et al. (2007) "Epidemiology of specific phobia subtypes: Findings from the Dresden Mental Health Study." *European Psychiatry 22*, 2, 69–74.

Benjamin, J., Ben-Zion, I.Z., Karbofsky, E., and Dannon, P. (2000) "Double-blind placebo-controlled pilot study of paroxetine for specific phobia." *Psychopharmacology 149*, 2, 194–196.

Berryhill, M.B., Halli-Tierney, A., Culmer, N., Williams, N., et al. (2018) "Videoconferencing psychological therapy and anxiety: A systematic review." *Family Practice 36*, 1, 53–63.

Bogusch, L.M., Moeller, M.T., and O'Brien, W.H. (2018) "Case study of acceptance and commitment therapy and functional analysis for emetophobia." *Clinical Case Studies 17*, 2, 77–90.

Boschen, M.J. (2007) "Reconceptualizing emetophobia: A cognitive–behavioral formulation and research agenda." *Journal of Anxiety Disorders 21*, 3, 407–419.

Boschen, M.J., Veale, D., Ellison, N., and Reddell, T. (2013) "The emetopho-bia questionnaire (EmetQ-13): Psychometric validation of a measure of specific phobia of vomiting (emetophobia)." *Journal of Anxiety Disorders 27*, 7, 670–677.

Bouras, E.P., Vazquez Roque, M.I., and Aranda-Michel, J. (2013) "Gastropare-sis: From concepts to management." *Nutrition in Clinical Practice 28*, 437.

Brown, T.A., and Barlow, D.H. (1992) "Comorbidity among anxiety disorders: Implications for treatment and DSM-IV." *Journal of Consulting and Clinical Psychology 60*, 6, 835–844.

Canadian Pharmacists Association (2021) *Compendium of Pharmaceuticals and Specialties: The Canadian Drug Reference for Health Professionals*. Ottawa: Canadian Pharmaceutical Association.

Christie, A. (Host). (2020a) "Emetophobia therapist Peter Silin talks about his unique approach" (S1E15) [Audio podcast episode], December 17. In *Emetophobia Help with Anna Christie*. www.buzzsprout.com/1307773

Christie, A. (Host). (2020b) "CBT/exposure is NOT about licking your shoe!" (S1E17) [Audio podcast episode], December 31. In *Emetophobia Help with Anna Christie*. www.buzzsprout.com/1307773

Christie, A. (Host). (2021) "Drs. Veale and Keyes, authors of *Free Yourself from Emetophobia*." (S2E2) [Audio podcast episode], October 17. In *Emetophobia Help with Anna Christie*. www.buzzsprout.com/1307773

Cili, S., and Stopa, L. (2015) "Intrusive mental imagery in psychological disorders: Is the self the key to understanding maintenance?" *Frontiers in Psychiatry 6*. https://doi.org/10.3389/fpsyt.2015.00103

Craske, M.G. (1999) *Anxiety Disorders: Psychological Approaches to Theory and Treatment*. Boulder, CO: Westview Press.

Craske, M.G., Street, L.L., Jayaraman, J., and Barlow, D.H. (1991) "Attention versus distraction during in vivo exposure: Snake and spider phobias." *Journal of Anxiety Disorders 5*, 3, 199–211.

Craske, M.G., Treanor, M., Conway, C.C., Zbozinek, T., et al. (2014) "Max-imizing exposure therapy: An inhibitory learning approach." *Behaviour Research and Therapy 58*, 10–23.

Crocq, M.A. (2015) "A history of anxiety: From Hippocrates to DSM." *Dia-logues in Clinical Neuroscience 17*, 3, 319–325.

Crohn's and Colitis Federation of America (2020) *The Facts about Irri-table Bowel Diseases Booklet*, 4–14. Accessed on 15/8/20 at www.crohnscolitisfoundation.org/science-and-professionals/patient-resources/patient-brochures

Dargis, M., and Burk, L. (2018) "A transdiagnostic approach to the treatment of emetophobia: A single case study." *Clinical Case Studies 18*, 1, 69–82.

Dattilio, F.M. (2003) "Emetic exposure and desensitization procedures in the reduction of nausea and a fear of emesis." *Clinical Case Studies 2*, 3, 199–210.

Davidson, A.L., Boyle, C., and Lauchlan, F. (2007) "Scared to lose control? General and health locus of control in females with a phobia of vomiting." *Journal of Clinical Psychology 64*, 1, 30–39.

de Jongh, A. (2012) "Treatment of a woman with emetophobia: A trauma focused approach." *Mental Illness 4*, 1, e3.

de Jongh, A., and ten Broeke, E. (1994) "Notable changes after one session of eye movement desensitization and reprocessing: A case of fear of nausea and vomiting." *Directieve Therapie 14*, 2, 46–52.

de Jongh, A., ten Broeke, E., and Renssen, M. (1999) "Treatment of specific phobias with eye movement desensitization and reprocessing (EMDR)." *Journal of Anxiety Disorders 13*, 1–2, 69–85.

Dosanjh, S., Fleisher, W., and Sam, D. (2017) "I think I'm going to be sick: An eight-year-old boy with emetophobia and secondary food restriction." *Journal of the Canadian Academy of Child and Adolescent Psychiatry 26*, 2, 104.

Ehlers, A., and Clark, D. (2000) "A cognitive model of posttraumatic stress disorder." *Behavior Research and Therapy 38*, 4, 319–345.

Enweluzo, C., and Aziz, F. (2013) "Gastroparesis: A review of current and emerging treatment options." *Clinical and Experimental Gastroenterology 6*, 161–165.

Faye, A.D., Gawande, S., Tadke, R., Kirpekar, V.C., et al. (2013) "Emetophobia: A fear of vomiting." *Indian Journal of Psychiatry 55*, 4, 390.

Fix, R.L., Proctor, K.B., and Gray, W.N. (2016) "Treating emetophobia and panic symptoms in an adolescent female: A case study." *Clinical Case Studies 15*, 4, 326–338.

Foa, E.B., and Kozak, M.J. (1986) "Emotional processing of fear: Exposure to corrective information." *Psychological Bulletin 99*, 1, 20–35.

Gan, T.J., Diemunsch, P., Habib, A.S., Kovac, A., et al. (2014) "Consensus guidelines for the management of postoperative nausea and vomiting." *Anesthesia and Analgesia 118*, 1, 85–113.

Gellatly, R., and Beck, A.T. (2016) "Catastrophic thinking: A transdiagnostic process across psychiatric disorders." *Cognitive Therapy and Research 40*, 4, 441–452.

Ghandour, R.M., Sherman, L.J., Vladutiu, C.J., Ali, M.M., et al. (2019) "Prevalence and treatment of depression, anxiety, and conduct problems in US children." *The Journal of Pediatrics 206*, 256–267.

Handwerk, B. (2017) "What stinky cheese tells us about the science of disgust." *Smithsonian Magazine*, Oct 3. Accessed on 13/08/22 at www. smithsonianmag.com/science-nature/what-stinky-cheese-tells-us-about-disgust-180965017

Höller, Y., Overveld, M.V., Jutglar, H., and Trinka, E. (2013) "Nausea in specific phobia of vomiting." *Behavioral Science 3*, 3, 445–458.

Huebner, D. (2007) *What to Do When your Brain Gets Stuck: A Kid's Guide to Overcoming OCD*. (Matthews, B., Illus.). Washington, DC: Magination Press.

Hunter, P.V., and Antony, M.M. (2009) "Cognitive-behavioral treatment of emetophobia: The role of interoceptive exposure." *Cognitive and Behavioral Practice 16*, 1, 84–91.

Huynh, D.T., Shamash, K., Burch, M., Phillips, E., et al. (2019) "Median arcuate ligament syndrome and its associated conditions." *The American Surgeon 85*, 1162–1165.

Infantino, A., Donovan, C.L., and March, S. (2016) "A randomized controlled trial of an audio-based treatment program for child anxiety disorders." *Behaviour Research and Therapy 79*, 35–45.

Jung, R.E., Flores, R.A., and Hunter, D. (2016) "A new measure of imagination ability: Anatomical brain imaging correlates." *Frontiers in Psychology 7*, April.

Kannappan, A., and Middleman, A.B. (2020) "Emetophobia: A case of nausea leading to dehydration in an adolescent female." *SAGE Open Medical Case Reports 8*, 2050313X20951335.

Kartsounis, L., Mervyn-Smith, J., and Pickersgill, M.J. (1983) "Factor analysis of the responses of British university students to the Fear Survey Schedule (FSS-III)." *Personality and Individual Differences 4*, 2, 157–163.

Kerr, C. (2013) "TA treatment of emetophobia: A hermeneutic single-case efficacy design study—'Peter.'" *International Journal of Transactional Analysis Research & Practice 4*, 2.

Keyes, A., and Veale, D. (2021) *Free Yourself from Emetophobia: A CBT Self-Help Guide for a Fear of Vomiting*. London: Jessica Kingsley Publishers.

Keyes, A., Gilpin, H.R., and Veale, D. (2018) "Phenomenology, epidemiology, co-morbidity and treatment of a specific phobia of vomiting: A systematic review of an understudied disorder." *Clinical Psychology Review 60*, 15–31.

Keyes, A., Deale, A., Foster, C., and Veale, D. (2020) "Time intensive cognitive behavioral therapy for a specific phobia of vomiting: A single case experimental design." *Journal of Behavior Therapy and Experimental Psychiatry 66*, 101523.

Kia, L., and Hirano, I. (2015) "Distinguishing GERD from eosinophilic oesophagitis: Concepts and controversies." *Nature Reviews Gastroenterology & Hepatology 12*, 379–386.

Kirkpatrick, D.R., and Berg, A.J. (1981) "Fears of a heterogenous nonpsychiatric sample: A factor analytic study." Paper presented at the *89th Annual Convention of the American Psychological Association*, Los Angeles, CA, August 24–26.

Lang, P.J., McTeague, L.M., and Bradley, M.M. (2016) "RDoC, DSM, and the reflex physiology of fear: A biodimensional analysis of the anxiety disorders spectrum." *Psychophysiology 53*, 3, 336–347.

Levey, D.F., Gelernter, J., Polimanti, R., Zhou, H., et al. (2020) "Reproducible genetic risk loci for anxiety: Results From ~200,000 participants in the Million Veteran Program." *American Journal of Psychiatry 177*, 3, 223–232.

Linehan, M.M. (1987) "Dialectical behavior therapy for borderline personality disorder: Theory and method." *Bulletin of the Menninger Clinic 51*, 3, 261–276.

Lippl, F., Hannig, C., Weiss, W., Allescher, H.D., et al. (2002) "Superior mesenteric artery syndrome: Diagnosis and treatment from the gastroenterologist's view." *Journal of Gastroenterology 37*, 8, 640–643.

Lipsitz, J.D., Fyer, A.J., Paterniti, A., and Klein, D.F. (2001) "Emetophobia: Preliminary results of an internet survey." *Depression & Anxiety 14*, 2, 149–152.

Lovitz, D., and Yusko, D. (2021) *Gag Reflections: Conquering a Fear of Vomit through Exposure Therapy*. Jefferson, NC: McFarland.

Lydiard, R.B., Laraia, M.T., Howell, E.F., and Ballenger, J.C. (1986) "Can panic disorder present as irritable bowel syndrome?" *The Journal of Clinical Psychiatry 47*, 9, 470–473.

Maack, D.J., Deacon, B.J., and Zhao, M. (2013) "Exposure therapy for emetophobia: A case study with three-year follow-up." *Journal of Anxiety Disorders 27*, 5, 527–534.

Maack, D.J., Ebesutani, C., and Smitherman, T.A. (2017) "Psychometric investigation of the specific phobia of vomiting inventory: A new factor model." *International Journal of Methods in Psychiatric Research 27*, 1, e1574.

Madjunkova, S., Maltepe, C., and Koren, G. (2014) "The delayed-release combination of doxylamine and pyridoxine (Diclegis®/Diclectin®) for the treatment of nausea and vomiting of pregnancy." *Pediatric Drugs 16*, 3, 199–211.

Manassis, K., and Kalman, E. (1990) "Anorexia resulting from fear of vomiting in four adolescent girls." *The Canadian Journal of Psychiatry 35*, 6, 548–550.

Mayo Clinic (2019) *Atypical Antidepressants*. Accessed on 10/6/22 at www.mayoclinic.org/diseases-conditions/depression/in-depth/atypical-antidepressants/art-20048208

Mayo Clinic (2022) *Irritable Bowel Syndrome—Symptoms and Causes*. Accessed on 31/10/22 at https://www.mayoclinic.org/diseases-conditions/irritable-bowel-syndrome/symptoms-causes/syc-20360016

McKenzie, S. (1994) "Hypnotherapy for vomiting phobia in a 40-year-old woman." *Contemporary Hypnosis* 11, 1, 37–40.

Mind (2020) *About Antipsychotics*. Accessed on 10/6/22 at www.mind.org.uk/information-support/drugs-and-treatments/antipsychotics/about-antipsychotics

Mitamura, T. (2019) "Case study of clinical behavior analysis for a 20-year-old patient with emetophobia." *Clinical Case Studies 18*, 3, 163–174.

Moran, D.J., and O'Brien, R.M. (2005) "Competence imagery: A case study treating emetophobia." *Psychological Reports 96*, 3, 1, 635–636.

Morrison, J. (2014) *DSM-5® Made Easy: The Clinician's Guide to Diagnosis*. New York: Guilford Press.

National Institute of Mental Health (2022) *Any Anxiety Disorder*. Accessed on 10/6/22 at www.nimh.nih.gov/health/statistics/any-anxiety-disorder

National Safety Council (2022) *Odds of Dying*. Accessed on 18/6/22 at https://injuryfacts.nsc.org/all-injuries/preventable-death-overview/odds-of-dying

Nuangchamnong, N., and Niebyl, J. (2014) "Doxylamine succinate-pyridoxine hydrochloride (Diclegis) for the management of nausea and vomiting in pregnancy: An overview." *International Journal of Women's Health 6*, 401–409.

Odze, R.D. (2009) "Pathology of eosinophilic esophagitis: What the clinician needs to know." *American Journal of Gastroenterology 104*, 485–490.

Olatunji, B.O., Deacon, B.J., and Abramowitz, J.S. (2009) "The cruelest cure? Ethical issues in the implementation of exposure-based treatments." *Cognitive and Behavioral Practice 16*, 2, 172–180.

Orme, K., Challacombe, F., and Roxborough, A. (2022) "Specific fear of vomiting (SPOV) in early parenthood: Assessment and treatment considerations with two illustrative cases." *The Cognitive Behavior Therapist 15*, E12.

Pandas Physicians Network (2022) *Pans Diagnostic Guidelines*. Accessed on 10/6/22 at www.pandasppn.org/pans

Perry, B., and Winfrey, O. (2021) *What Happened to You? Conversations on Trauma, Resilience, and Healing*. New York: Flatiron Books.

Philips, H. (1985) "Return of fear in the treatment of a fear of vomiting." *Behavior Research and Therapy 23*, 1, 45–52.

Preston, J.D., O'Neal, J.H., Talaga, M.C., and Moore, B.A. (2021) *Handbook of Clinical Psychopharmacology for Therapists, Ninth Edition*. Oakland, CA: New Harbinger Publications.

Price, K., Veale, D., and Brewin, C.R. (2012) "Intrusive imagery in people with a specific phobia of vomiting." *Journal of Behavior Therapy and Experimental Psychiatry 43*, 1, 672–678.

Rachman, S. (1977) "The conditioning theory of fear acquisition: A critical examination." *Behavior Research and Therapy 15*, 5, 375–387.

Reddan, M.C., Wager, T.D., and Schiller, D. (2018) "Attenuating neural threat expression with imagination." *Neuron 100*, 4, 994–1005.

Reneau, A. (2022) "Ever heard of emetophobia? The oddly common phobia that is often misdiagnosed as anxiety or anorexia." *Upworthy*, May 5. Accessed on 10/6/22 at www.upworthy.com/emetophobia-often-misdiagnosed-as-generalized-anxiety-or-anorexia

Riddle-Walker, L., Veale, D., Chapman, C., Ogle, F., et al. (2016) "Cognitive behavior therapy for specific phobia of vomiting (emetophobia): A pilot randomized controlled trial." *Journal of Anxiety Disorders 43*, 14–22.

Ritow, J.K. (1979) "Brief treatment of a vomiting phobia." *American Journal of Clinical Hypnosis 21*, 4, 293–296.

Russ, D., and McCarthy, C. (2010) *Turnaround: Turning Fear into Freedom*. Charlotte, NC: Informed Therapy Resources.

Russ, D., and McCarthy, C. (2016) *Emetophobia Supplement*. Charlotte, NC: Informed Therapy Resources.

Salkovskis, P.M. (1996) "The cognitive approach to anxiety: Threat beliefs, safety-seeking behaviour, and the special case of health anxiety and obsessions." In P.M. Salkovskis (ed.) *Frontiers of Cognitive Therapy* (pp. 48–75). New York: Guilford Press.

Simons, M., and Vloet, T.D. (2018) "Emetophobia—A metacognitive therapeutic approach for an overlooked disorder." *Zeitschrift für Kinder- und Jugendpsychiatrie und Psychotherapie 46*, 1, 57–66.

Song, L., and Foster, C. (2022) "Patients' and therapists' experiences of CBT videoconferencing in anxiety disorders." *The Cognitive Behavior Therapist 15*, E14.

Spergel, J.M., Dellon, E.S., Liacouras, C.A., Hirano, I., et al. (2018) "Summary of the updated international consensus diagnostic criteria for eosinophilic esophagitis." *Annals of Allergy, Asthma & Immunology 121*, 3, 281–284.

Spijker, J., Muntingh, A., and Batelaan, N. (2020) "Advice for clinicians on how to treat comorbid anxiety and depression." *JAMA Psychiatry 77*, 6, 645.

Stampfl, T.G., and Levis, D.J. (1967) "Essentials of implosive therapy: A learning-theory-based psychodynamic behavioral therapy." *Journal of Abnormal Psychology 72*, 6, 496–503.

Stein, B., Everhart, K.K., and Lacy, B.E. (2015) "Gastroparesis." *Journal of Clinical Gastroenterology 49*, 7, 550–558.

Stubbings, D.R., Rees, C.S., Roberts, L.D., and Kane, R.T. (2013) "Comparing in-person to videoconference-based cognitive behavioral therapy for mood and anxiety disorders: Randomized controlled trial." *Journal of Medical Internet Research 15*, 11, e258.

Sung, J.J., Chung, S.C., Ling, T.K., Yung, M.Y., et al. (1995) "Antibacterial treatment of gastric ulcers associated with helicobacter pylori." *New England Journal of Medicine 332*, 139–142.

Swedo, S.E., Leonard, H.L., Garvey, M., Mittleman, B., et al. (1998) "Pediatric autoimmune neuropsychiatric disorders associated with streptococcal infections: Clinical description of the first 50 cases." *American Journal of Psychiatry 155*, 2, 264–271.

Swedo, S.E., Seidlitz, J., Kovacevic, M., Latimer, M.E., et al. (2015) "Clinical presentation of pediatric autoimmune neuropsychiatric disorders associated with streptococcal infections in research and community settings." *Journal of Child and Adolescent Psychopharmacology 25*, 1, 26–30.

Sykes, M., Boschen, M.J., and Conlon, E.G. (2016) "Comorbidity in emetophobia (specific phobia of vomiting)." *Clinical Psychology & Psychotherapy 23*, 4, 363–367.

Van Hout, W.J., and Bouman, T.K. (2011) "Clinical features, prevalence and psychiatric complaints in subjects with fear of vomiting." *Clinical Psychology and Psychotherapy 19*, 6, 531–539.

Van Overveld, M., De Jong, P.J., Peters, M.L., Van Hout, W.J., and Bouman, T.K. (2008) "An internet-based study on the relation between disgust sensitivity and emetophobia." *Journal of Anxiety Disorders 22*, 3, 524–531.

Veale, D. (2009) "Cognitive behavior therapy for a specific phobia of vomiting." *The Cognitive Behavior Therapist 2*, 4, 272–288.

Veale, D., and Lambrou, C. (2006) "The psychopathology of vomit phobia." *Behavioral and Cognitive Psychotherapy 34*, 2, 139–150.

Veale, D., Costa, A., Murphy, P., and Ellison, N. (2012) "Abnormal eating behavior in people with a specific phobia of vomiting (emetophobia)." *European Eating Disorders Review 20*, 5, 414–418.

Veale, D., Ellison, N., Boschen, M.J., Costa, A., et al. (2013a) "Development of an inventory to measure specific phobia of vomiting (emetophobia)." *Cognitive Therapy and Research 37*, 3, 595–604.

Veale, D., Murphy, P., Ellison, N., Kanakam, N., and Costa, A. (2013b) "Autobiographical memories of vomiting in people with a specific phobia of vomiting (emetophobia)." *Journal of Behavior Therapy and Experimental Psychiatry 44*, 1, 14–20.

Veale, D., Hennig, C., and Gledhill, L. (2015) "Is a specific phobia of vomiting part of the obsessive compulsive and related disorders?" *Journal of Obsessive-Compulsive and Related Disorders 7*, 1–6.

Verwoerd, J., Van Hout, W.J., and De Jong, P.J. (2016) "Disgust- and anxiety-based emotional reasoning in non-clinical fear of vomiting." *Journal of Behavior Therapy and Experimental Psychiatry 50*, 83–89.

Whitton, S.W., Luiselli, J.K., and Donaldson, D.L. (2006) "Cognitive-behavioral treatment of generalized anxiety: Disorder and vomiting phobia in an elementary-age child." *Clinical Case Studies 5*, 6, 477–487.

Wijesinghe, B. (1974) "A vomiting phobia overcome by one session of flooding with hypnosis." *Journal of Behavior Therapy and Experimental Psychiatry 5*, 2, 169–170.

Wu, M.S., Selles, R.R., Novoa, J.C., Zepeda, R., et al. (2016) "Examination of the phenomenology and clinical correlates of emetophobia in a sample of Salvadorian youths." *Child Psychiatry & Human Development 48*, 3, 509–516.

Zafarmand, M., Farahmand, Z., and Otared, N. (2022) "A systematic literature review and meta-analysis on effectiveness of neurofeedback for obsessive-compulsive disorder." *Neurocase 28*, 1, 29–36.

Zimerman, A., and Doan, H.M. (2003) "Prenatal attachment and other feelings and thoughts during pregnancy in three groups of pregnant women." *Journal of Prenatal and Perinatal Psychology and Health 18*, 131–148.

# Subject Index

# Author Index